TWO ON AN ISLAND

PLAYS

By ELMER RICE

❖

WE, THE PEOPLE

JUDGMENT DAY

TWO PLAYS:
Between Two Worlds
Not for Children

AMERICAN LANDSCAPE

TWO ON AN ISLAND

A Novel

IMPERIAL CITY

SCENE 2

All Around the Town

TWO ON AN ISLAND

A Play in Eleven Scenes by ELMER RICE

COWARD-McCANN, INC.

NEW YORK, 1940

MANUFACTURED IN THE UNITED STATES OF AMERICA

At the Van Rees Press, New York

The cast of the play as originally presented by

THE PLAYWRIGHTS' COMPANY

MAXWELL ANDERSON   S. N. BEHRMAN   ELMER RICE
ROBERT SHERWOOD

at the Broadhurst Theater, New York City.
January 22, 1940

◇

TWO ON AN ISLAND
A New Play in Eleven Scenes

BY ELMER RICE

Staged by the Author

Designed and lighted by JO MIELZINER
Costumes by HELENE PONS

CHARACTERS
(In the order of their appearance)

Character	*Played by*
WILLIAM FLYNN	ROBERT WILLIAMS
SAMUEL BRODSKY	MARTIN RITT
A REDCAP	EARL SYDNOR
MARY WARD	BETTY FIELD
JOHN THOMPSON	JOHN CRAVEN
A POLICEMAN	EDWARD DOWNES
CLIFTON ROSS	EARL McDONALD
THE SIGHTSEEING GUIDE	HOWARD daSILVA
THE DRIVER	ROBERT O'BRIEN
MRS. DORA LEVY	DORA WEISSMAN
DIXIE BUSHBY	ARTHUR L. SACHS
A MIDDLE-WESTERN MAN	RODERICK MAYBEE
A MIDDLE-WESTERN WOMAN	ROBERTA BELLINGER

32117

Character	*Played by*
FREDERIC WINTHROP	WHITNER BISSELL
LAWRENCE ORMONT	LUTHER ADLER
MARTHA JOHNSON	TERRY HARRIS
AN ACTOR	CHARLES POLACHECK
HEINZ KALTBART	RUDOLF WEISS
DOROTHY CLARK	MARTHA HODGE
KATHERINE WINTHROP HOLMES	JOAN WETMORE
MARTIN BLAKE	HERSCHEL BENTLEY
A CASHIER	NORMA GREEN
GRACIE MULLEN	ANN THOMAS
A MARRIED COUPLE	{ SARA PEYTON { JOHN PHILLIBER
HELEN ORMONT	HARRIET MACGIBBON
SONIA TARANOVA	EVA LANGBORD
MRS. BALLINGER	FREDERICA GOING
A MUSEUM ATTENDANT	CHARLES LA TORRE
ANOTHER MARRIED COUPLE	{ JOHN TRIGGS { DOROTHY DARLING
RUTH ORMONT	HELEN RENEE
A HINDU	LARRI LAURIA
A WAITER	AAGE STEENSHORNE
ANOTHER MARRIED COUPLE	{ SELLWYN MYERS { LUCILLE SEARS
FRED	DON SHELTON
DOLLY	ADELE LONGMIRE
MRS. WILLIAMS	MARY MICHAEL

NEW YORKERS AND OUT-OF-TOWNERS: Roberta Bellinger, Alvin Childress, Dorothy Darling, Evelyn Davis, Virginia Girvin, Frederica Going, Terry Harris, Eva Langbord, Charles La Torre, Larri Lauria, Adele Longmire, Assotta Marshall, Roderick Maybee, Sellwyn Myers, Mary Michael, Robert O'Brien, Sara Peyton, John Philliber, Hilary Phillips, Arthur L. Sachs, Lucille Sears, Don Shelton, Aage Steenshorne, Earl Sydnor, Joan Wetmore, Robert Williams.

ACT ONE

Scene 1

Two taxicabs face the audience head on and side by side. The one at the left is rather dingy and decrepit—the independent-owner type of cab. The one at the right is a bright and shiny unit of one of the large fleets. WILLIAM FLYNN, *the driver at the left, is a brawny, thick-necked fellow in need of a shave. He is chewing the stump of a cigar and divides his attention between his radio and a tabloid.* SAMUEL BRODSKY, *the driver at the right, is small and slight but wiry and tough. He wears thick-lensed glasses. He is listening to his radio, also, and making notes in a large notebook.*

FLYNN'S RADIO

And now, ladies and gentlemen, the makers of Goodie Goods, the power-plus breakfast cereal, take you once again to the Congo Room atop the Hotel Metropolitan, where Mel Bigelow and his Mad Merrymakers will interpret for you in their own inimitable way some of your favorite songs. For an opening number they present that seductive tune, *Love Walked In*. And now for Mel Bigelow and his Mad Merrymakers.

(*The music begins.*)

BRODSKY'S RADIO

(*Simultaneously*)

But, though most of our gay songsters begin to flit southward when the bright autumn leaves flutter to the ground and the nights grow chilly, there are some hardier fellows

among them who cling loyally to their beloved northern
homes and whose stout hearts are not daunted, even by
the rigors of a New England winter. If you have patience
and sharp eyes, you are likely to see quite a variety of
gaily feathered little friends. Bold, bright-eyed little chicka-
dees, in their smart black and gray dinner jackets, trooping
in threes and fours; showy, crested bluejays, big fellows
at once arrogant and timid; serious, businesslike little nut-
hatches; a purple finch, maybe; or, if you are lucky, a
downy woodpecker or his bigger cousin, the hairy woodpecker.

(*During the foregoing a* NEGRO REDCAP *enters at the
right, carrying a large suitcase to which an umbrella is
strapped, and a smaller wicker bag. He is followed by*
MARY WARD, *a pretty girl of twenty, attractively but not
fashionably dressed. The* REDCAP *opens the door of the
cab and puts the bags inside, while* BRODSKY *switches off
his radio, puts away his notebook, and waits for instruc-
tions.*)

THE REDCAP

O.K., miss.

MARY

Thank you.
(*She fumbles in her purse.*)
Oh, dear! Have you got change of a quarter?

THE REDCAP

Change of a quarter? No, miss, I ain't.

MARY

Oh, well, maybe the driver—no, wait a minute, I think I
have it right here. Yes, here's a nickel—

THE REDCAP

I can't change that, neither.

MARY

(*Laughing*)

No, of course not! And I'm sure I have five pennies. Yes, one, two, three, four, five. I hope you don't mind pennies.

THE REDCAP

I didn't know they was still making them. I sure do thank you, miss.

MARY

Oh, you're welcome.

THE REDCAP

Good night, miss, good night. Have a good time and don't spend all your money in one place.

MARY

(*Laughing*)

No, don't worry, I won't!

THE REDCAP

(*Jingling the coins, as he walks away*)

Boy, oh boy! Fistful of dough and tomorrow's my day off!

BRODSKY

(*Putting down his flag and starting his engine*)

What destination?

MARY

I'd like to go to the Y.W.C.A., please.

BRODSKY

Any particular branch?

MARY

Oh, is there more than one? Well, I really don't know. I've never been in New York before. I'm looking for a place to live.

BRODSKY

My suggestion is the Central Branch.

MARY

Can I get a nice room there?

BRODSKY

Modest accommodations for Gentile young women, I'm told. Naturally, I've never been inside.

MARY

That's exactly what I'm looking for. Something clean and simple.

BRODSKY

Well, we'll try the Central Branch. I was acquainted, at one time, with a young lady who lived at the Y.W.*H*.A. but that won't do you any good. And could she play the cello! I don't exaggerate when I say that her andantes would tear your heartstrings.

(*Meanwhile* JOHN THOMPSON *enters at the left. He is a tall, broad-shouldered boy in his early twenties. His cheap, ready-made clothes are crumpled and travel-stained. He carries a large, battered valise, a tennis racket, and a portable typewriter.*)

JOHN

Are you busy?

FLYNN

Not till you get in.

(*He switches off his radio and starts his engine.*)

JOHN

All right, I'll get in then. I want to go to the Y.M.C.A.

FLYNN

Which one?

JOHN

Gosh, you've got me. Wherever I can get a room and shower. I've been riding in a day coach since yesterday morning and I've got a load of coal dust I want to get rid of.

FLYNN

How about the West Side Branch?

JOHN

I wouldn't know one from the other. It's my first time in New York. The West Side Branch sounds all right to me.

FLYNN

You wouldn't be a member of the Knights of Columbus?

JOHN

Why, no, I'm not. Who are they?

FLYNN

(*Giving him a scornful glance*)

O.K., West Side Branch.

MARY

(*Looking about eagerly*)

Why, this is wonderful—with the top open like this. You can see everything. What a nice way to build a taxi.

BRODSKY

Well, you have to give them luxury these days if you want the business. We're living in an age of cut-throat competition.

MARY

Goodness, look at the size of the buildings. What are they, apartment houses?

BRODSKY

That's right. The cliff dwellings of the modern Babylonia.

MARY

What's it called, this street?

BRODSKY

Park Avenue. You've heard of it, no doubt?

MARY

I most certainly have! Park Avenue—my!

BRODSKY

The street of good dogs and bad women, as the saying is.

MARY

(*Laughing*)

I never heard that before. But don't the four hundred live here? The Vanderbilts and the Astors and all those?

BRODSKY

That's a mistaken idea that out-of-town folks have. Our old families prefer the quiet dignity of the side streets. Nobody lives here but a lot of social climbers and nouveau rich. Ostentation but no class.

JOHN

Well, I'm on Manhattan Island at last! I've been dreaming about this ever since I was a kid and now I'm here. I thought I had a pretty good idea of it, from the movies and the rotogravures, but you really have to see it to believe it.

FLYNN

Yeah, they all fall for it.

JOHN

Do you ever get used to it?

FLYNN

How's that?

JOHN

All this, I mean! New York! Does the excitement ever

wear off? I guess it must, after a while, but I hope it doesn't.

FLYNN

Well, it's a tough place to make a livin'. There's too many hacks on the streets. At that, it's better than Boston. That's my home town.

JOHN

Is that so? I must have some third or fourth cousins living up there. My family originally came from Massachusetts— about a hundred years ago, that is. Thompson.

FLYNN

That don't mean nothin'. There's about as many Thompsons in Boston as Flynns. My old man came over from County Kerry. He got killed fallin' off a scaffoldin', one mornin' after a wake.

JOHN

Well, my father got caught in a blizzard, about five years ago, and died of pneumonia. We get some pretty tough winters out there in Iowa, where I come from.

FLYNN

Yeah? Well, when you get west of the Hudson, it's all the same to me.

MARY

Oh, this is too wonderful for words. Why, I can even see some stars. Just imagine seeing the stars over New York! I had no idea you ever could.

BRODSKY

And yet, how many ever raise their eyes to look at them? Do you know what the curse of this modern age is! Materialism! No time for poetry.

MARY

Yes, I suppose that's true of city life. But you see, I grew up in the country and the stars are part of your life there, like trees and running water. There's a big red one—

BRODSKY

Mars.

MARY

I thought it must be. I've never seen it so big and bright!

BRODSKY

At this moment, it's closer to the earth than it's been in seventeen years.

(*He suddenly jams on his brakes.*)

MARY

(*Almost jounced out of her seat*)

Oh!

BRODSKY

Woman driver! Of all the planets, Mars is the most favorably situated for observation from the earth. And, furthermore, it presents the most interesting surface features.

MARY

You know a lot, don't you?

BRODSKY

I'm a bookworm. Reading maketh a full man, says Lord Beaconsfield. I'm wasting my time driving a hack. But when you consider present economic conditions today—

JOHN

Which way are we going now—north?

FLYNN

Yeah. Uptown.

JOHN

That's what I thought. I tried to buy a map of New York

in the railroad station in Chicago. But all I got from the fellow at the newsstand was a dirty look. I guess I must have wounded his civic pride. Say, it's a wonderful idea, having the streets numbered like this. Must make it easy to find your way around.

FLYNN

Manhattan's all right. But wait till you get up in the East Bronx. Even the cops get lost, once they get off their beats.

MARY

Do you think it's true that Mars is inhabited?

BRODSKY

Absolutely without scientific foundation. Just a lot of notoriety seekers, preying upon the guilability of the public. Like those cosmic rays you read about in the Hearst press. Nothing but figments of the imagination. That's the Waldorf.

MARY

Oh, is it? Look at the size of it! It must be simply beautiful inside.

BRODSKY

A self-contained city. You could live your whole life there without ever setting foot outside. Yeah, the credibility of some people. You can hardly believe it. Like that radio broadcast a couple of years ago about the air raid from Mars.

MARY

Oh, yes. That actor, what was his name?

BRODSKY

For the moment, you've got me nonplussed. Oh, yeah, Wells. That's it. H. G. Wells.

MARY

Oh, no, not H. G. He's a writer.

BRODSKY

That was the name all right—H. G. Wells. I have an encyclopediac memory—the result of long training. But maybe I'm wrong at that.

JOHN

What street is this we're on now?

FLYNN

Eighth Avenue. Theayter district.

JOHN

(*Excitedly*)

Theater district? Where? I don't see any theaters.

FLYNN

Down the side streets, on your right.

JOHN

Oh, yes, I see them. Katharine Cornell! I saw her in *Romeo and Juliet* in Des Moines. Say, this is pretty thrilling. That's the first thing I'm going to do—go to a New York theater. What's the best show in town?

FLYNN

I couldn't tell you. I don't follow the theayter. All I do is drop 'em on the sidewalk and pick 'em up when the show is over. The Music Box is where they're all goin' now.

(*To another driver*)

Go on, go on. What do you think you're doin', the rhumba?

(*Disgustedly, to* JOHN)

Joisey!

BRODSKY

You from upstate?

MARY

No, New Hampshire. A little town called Laconia. I suppose you're a New Yorker?

BRODSKY

An adopted son. I was born in Galicia.

MARY

Where's that? In Europe?

BRODSKY

It used to be in Poland or Austria-Hungaria. I don't know where it is now.

FLYNN

There's the Garden, right there.

JOHN

Oh, yes, Madison Square Garden!

FLYNN

That's where the big fight is tonight. Mike Dorando versus Sailor Kline.

JOHN

Yes, I know.

FLYNN

The main bout'll go on in about ten minutes now. Boy, I sure would like to be sittin' in one of them ringside seats, instead of pushin' this old boiler around.

JOHN

Well, I wouldn't mind being there myself. That's another thing I'll have to do—take in a fight. I want to see everything that this town has to offer. Who's going to win?

FLYNN

Well, I got my dough on Sailor Kline. If the little mockie don't come t'rough, I'm out five bucks. I was a goddam good middle-weight myself one time.

JOHN

You were? Did you ever fight at the Garden?

FLYNN

No. I was only a semi-pro. But two years runnin', I was middle-weight champeen o' the Mutual Welfare League.

BRODSKY

Here we are.

MARY

Oh, are we here already? What a shame! I never had such an exciting ride in my life. Well, it looks like a nice place.

BRODSKY

(Getting out and opening the door)

Conventional, both in its architecture and its policies.

MARY

How much do I owe you?

BRODSKY

Half a dollar.

MARY

Goodness, I guess I won't be taking many taxis.

(She gives him two coins.)

Twenty-five, fifty, is that right?

BRODSKY

Absolutely. With me the fair sex is always right. I'll take the bags in for you.

MARY

Oh, thank you very much. You made the ride very interesting for me.

BRODSKY

Don't mention it. According to my philosophy, a little chivalry is not amiss in the sordid life of the metropolis.

MARY

Why, everybody I've talked to has been just so nice to me.
I had no idea New Yorkers were so friendly.

BRODSKY

The appeal of feminine beauty is universal.
   (*He takes up the bags and she follows him off right.*)

FLYNN

O.K.

JOHN

Oh, is this it? How much is it?

FLYNN

Seventy.

JOHN

Seventy? Phew!
   (*He hands him a dollar bill.*)
Say, it looks all right.

FLYNN

   (*Giving him change*)
And twenty is a buck.

JOHN

Didn't you say seventy?

FLYNN

And the tip.

JOHN

   (*Confused*)
Oh, sure, of course.
   (*He picks up his bags and starts to go off left.*)

FLYNN

Say, Doc, how would you feel about havin' a good time
tonight?

JOHN

A good time?

(*Comprehending*)

Oh! Well, thanks, but I've got to get a shower and some sleep.

FLYNN

Well, here's my card. William Flynn. Anytime you feel like havin' a little entertainment, give me a buzz. All it'll cost you is five bucks and it'll be good.

JOHN

Thanks. I'll remember that. Good night.

FLYNN

Good night.

(JOHN *exits left with his bags.* FLYNN *switches on his radio.* BRODSKY, *meanwhile, has returned to his cab and switched on his radio.*)

FLYNN'S RADIO

And here's the bell for the second round. Both boys are still fresh and look ready for action. Mike has a bad bruise under his right eye where that hard right of the Sailor's landed in the first round but he seems none the worse for it. He tries a hard left to the Sailor's jaw but it's short. He tries again but the Sailor takes it on his shoulder. Kline tries a short jab to the body and another but that old defense of Mike's is working and he covers up. They're in the middle of the ring now, trading body punches, but they're light and there's no damage. Now they're working over to a neutral corner and they go into a clinch. Referee Jim Andrews separates them and they're back in the middle of the ring, waltzing around each other and trading light punches. The crowd is getting sore, whistling and booing and yelling "Give us some action! Go on and fight!" Now the Sailor is driving Mike back into his corner. He keeps trying for the Dago's jaw but they're all short. There, that one landed! But Mike is right back with two hard lefts to the body and now a right.

BRODSKY'S RADIO

(Simultaneously)

Harlan, Kentucky—The Governor proclaimed martial law today in a determined effort to bring to an end the bloody warfare between striking coal miners and company guards, which has already taken a toll of seven lives. Williamsport, Pennsylvania.—Flood waters continued to rise here today and authorities predicted that the peak would not be reached for another twenty-four hours. Twenty-seven bodies have already been recovered and the property loss is put at several million. Galesburg, Illinois.—Armed bandits today staged a daring raid on the Second National Bank and escaped with two hundred thousand dollars in cash and negotiable securities. Charles Hoffman, a teller, who attempted resistance, was shot in the abdomen and later died of his wounds. Vicksburg, Mississippi.—The Chief of Police announced today that he was unable to identify the leaders of a mob which last Thursday lynched and burned Joe Bostwick, a Negro, charged with attacking a white woman. Columbus, Ohio.—William McLaughlin was today indicted for first degree murder. Last Friday, McLaughlin shot and killed his wife, Rosalind, and George Patterson, wealthy drinking-cup manufacturer, with whom McLaughlin claimed she had been intimate.

(*In the middle of this there is a screeching of brakes and a crash of metal as the two cabs presumably collide. The radios continue throughout.*)

FLYNN

(*Jumping out of his cab*)

Hey, you mugg, where the hell do you think you're goin'?

BRODSKY

(*Jumping out of his cab*)

You big gorilla! Why don't you consult an optician?

FLYNN

Don't give me none of that, you cockeyed little bastard, or I'll smack you down.

BRODSKY

You and what army, tough guy?

FLYNN

Take off them cheaters, you lousy little heel, and I'll show you.

BRODSKY

Shut your hatch, Tarzan, you're creating a draft.

(*During this, a* POLICEMAN *comes up and begins to take part in the discussion, but a growing chorus of automobile horns makes it impossible to hear what any of them is saying. The* MEN *are talking volubly and gesticulating violently, the radios are going full blast, and there is a swelling crescendo of automobile horns, radio cars, sirens, ambulance bells, and fire engine gongs, as the*

Curtain Falls

Scene 2

Diagonally across the stage is a sightseeing bus, facing downstage right. It is an open bus, without a top or superstructure, so that the occupants are plainly visible above the sides. There are five rows of seats, each row providing a single place on one side of the aisle and two places on the other. The light in the scene is concentrated entirely upon the bus, leaving the rest of the stage in darkness. At the rise of the curtain, the bus is about half full. On the double seat next to the rear is MRS. DORA LEVY, a pleasant-faced elderly woman in black. In the front seat is FREDERIC WINTHROP, young, slender, oversensitive, overintellectualized. He is reading the Daily Worker. *Behind him is a burly, middle-aged, middle-class MIDDLE-WESTERNER. Three or four assorted PASSENGERS are in the single seats on the upstage side. THE DRIVER is seated at the wheel, THE GUIDE stands beside the hood, waiting for more customers. A moment after the rise of the curtain DIXIE BUSHBY, a sailor from an American battleship, and a fellow SAILOR are entering the bus. As they take the double seat in front of MRS. LEVY, MARY enters from the right.*

MARY

Is this the Chinatown tour?

THE DRIVER

Yes, ma'am, it is.

THE GUIDE

Got your ticket, miss?

19

MARY

Yes.

THE GUIDE

Thanks. Step right into the limousine, miss, and make yourself at home.

(MARY *enters the bus.*)

MARY

(*To* MRS. LEVY)

Is this seat taken?

MRS. LEVY

No, no, sit down, sit down.

MARY

I was afraid I was going to be late.

MRS. LEVY

Well, I guess they don't always start right on the minute.

(TWO SOUTHERN GIRLS *enter from the right.*)

THE FIRST SOUTHERN GIRL

Is this where we get the bus for the sightseeing tour?

THE GUIDE

You bet it is. We're leaving any minute now. Tickets, please.

THE FIRST SOUTHERN GIRL

Can we get two seats alone by ourselves, where we can sit together?

THE GUIDE

(*Imitating her accent*)

Absolutely. There's two nice ones back there that I been holdin' for you.

THE FIRST SOUTHERN GIRL

Oh, I see, way back there. Do you think we should try those, Claiborne?

THE SECOND SOUTHERN GIRL

I reckon we might as well.

(*They enter the bus and take the vacant rear seats.* DIXIE *whispers something to his friend, who guffaws loudly.*)

MRS. LEVY

(*To* MARY)

You're a stranger in New York, too?

MARY

Yes, I am. I've only been here two days.

MRS. LEVY

Is that so? Only two days? Well, I'm here nearly a month now, so I thought I might as well see some of the sights.

MARY

Where is your home?

MRS. LEVY

Well, now it's in New York. For thirty-two years I lived in Elmira. My husband was in business there, the Emporium Dry Goods Store, but last January he passed away.

MARY

Oh, that's too bad.

MRS. LEVY

Well, that's the way it goes. Today we're here and tomorrow we're gone. So now I'm living here with my daughter and her husband.

MARY

And do you go around all by yourself?

MRS. LEVY

Of course, why not? I'm strong and I have my health and who's going to hurt an old lady? The young people are busy with their friends and their bridge games and so I find ways to amuse myself.

(CLIFTON ROSS, *an artist, about forty, enters from the right. He has a club-foot and wears a high shoe.*)

THE GUIDE

O.K., mister, step right in.

(ROSS *sits next to* WINTHROP. *Throughout the tour he makes rapid sketches of his fellow passengers on a sketch pad.*)

MRS. LEVY

Where do you live?

MARY

Well, I come from New Hampshire but I'm going to live here, too, now.

MRS. LEVY

You're a business girl?

MARY

No, I want to get a job on the stage.

(THE SAILORS *turn and stare at her.*)

MRS. LEVY

Oh, so you're an actress?

MARY

Well, I hope to be.

MRS. LEVY

That's wonderful. Maybe one of these days I'll go to a theater and I'll see you acting in a play.

MARY

Yes, I certainly hope you will.

THE GUIDE

(*Entering the bus*)

Well, I guess we're all set.

A WOMAN PASSENGER

Well, it's about time.

THE GUIDE

(*As he sees* JOHN *approaching at the right*)

Hurry up, mister. We're just goin' to pull in the gangplank.

JOHN

(*Hurrying on*)

I was afraid I wouldn't make it.

THE GUIDE

No, you're just in time.

(JOHN *enters the bus and takes the vacant seat beside the* MIDDLE-WESTERNER.)

THE GUIDE

(*To* THE DRIVER)

All right, Charlie, let's go.

(*He sits facing the passengers and addresses them through a megaphone. Throughout there is incidental music appropriate to the localities described.*)

Folks, on this trip visiting Fifth Avenue, Green Witch Village, the Bowery, Chinatown, the waterfront, Harlem, the Gay White Way—all those points of interest in the world's greatest city that you've all read about will tonight become a reality. Now, friends, we're gonna be together quite a while so make yourselves comfortable. Sit back and smoke if you wish and in case your feet are tired from walking around the town all day, take off your shoes. Now, I'd just like to point out that every day in the year, including Sundays and legal holidays, New York has a daily average of 115,000 visitors, a human influx equal in size to the entire population of Spokane, Washington, or Fort Wayne, Indiana. The world's greatest city, seven million six hundred thousand people, fifty-seven nationalities, fifty-seven varieties in the Heinz League of Nations, 21,000 policemen, 137 hospitals, 297,000 dogs, 500,000 cats, more or less, 638 churches, 15,000 taxicabs. Half the life of the city is spent ducking the taxicab drivers.

THE MIDDLE-WESTERNER

It sure is.

THE GUIDE

Forty-second Street we're on now, going east. Times Square, named after that great newspaper, the *New York Times*. On your left the Times Building, the only building in the world that has no foundation of its own, being built right on the sidewalk. Throughout this tour only the sky-scrapers over forty stories high will be pointed out to you. Anything less, we consider a bungalow. Manhattan Island is fourteen miles long, two and a hahf miles wide. You'll notice I say "hahf" because we're approaching Fifth Avenue. When we get to the Bowery, I'll say "haff." On your right, the New York Public Library, contains four million books, pamphlets and periodicals, exceeded only by the Congressional Library in Washington. Personally, I've only read two of the books, but they tell me the others are good, too. On the corner at your left, Tiffany's, handmade jewelry all made to order. Drop in tomorrow and get yourself measured for a square-cut emerald or a diamond tarara. Now, on your right, we are approaching the famous Empire State Building, also known as the Empty State Building—fifty per cent empty—the world's tallest building, 102 stories, 1052 feet high. Might as well look up, friends, because it costs you a dollar-ten to go up on top and look down.

THE MIDDLE-WESTERNER

(*To* JOHN)
You been up there?

JOHN

No, not yet. I've only been here two days.

THE MIDDLE-WESTERNER

I went up this afternoon. I've been up Radio City, too.

JOHN

Yes, I did that yesterday. Got a great thrill out of it, too.

THE MIDDLE-WESTERNER

Well, I'll tell you, the way I figure it, it's a wonderful
town to visit but I wouldn't live here if you gave me the
place.

THE GUIDE

On your left, that little church there is the Church of the
Transfiguration, better known as the Little Church Around
The Corner, the favorite church for theatrical folks to get
married in. Some of them like it so much that they come
back three or four times. The late Nat Goodwin, celebrated
comedian, came back seven times. What a man!

MRS. LEVY

Oh, of course, Nat Goodwin. I saw him when I was a
young girl. A wonderful actor.

THE GUIDE

Now, folks, on your left is Madison Square. Note the
flagpole topped by the Eternal Light and dedicated to the
men who made the supreme sacrifice in the first World
War. We are now passing through the wholesale clothing
district. The streets down here are known as the streets of
gold. Look right and left and note the signs. Goldstein—
Goldberg—Goldblatt. This is Fourteenth Street. Thirty-five

years ago this was the city's Gay White Way. On your left, not far from here, is the headquarters of Tammany Hall, formerly a powerful political organization. Note the sidewalk cafés and restaurants—just like Paris—where tired business men take their secretaries for lunch—with a bottle of wine. You can get a ham sandwich here for a dollar; with mustard, a dollar and a quarter. Ah, this is a great city. We are now passing through Washington Square, a park immortalized in song, poetry, and story. Once the home of Mark Twain and many other celebrated writers. Now the Bohemian section begins, the section of the artists. This section is known as Green Witch Village or, more familiarly to its habitués, as the Village. Green Witch Village, the gayest, maddest, most unique spot in New York, where women go hatless and men wear long hair....

(*Suddenly pointing*)

There's one right there on the corner!

(*The* PASSENGERS *all turn to look.*)

See the fellow with the long hair? We are now entering Little Italy, where spaghetti is sold by the yard. Those white knobs hanging outside the stores are garlic, the use of which is now forbidden by the rules of civilized warfare.

DIXIE

Wops!

THE OTHER SAILOR

Yeah.

THE GUIDE

On your right, the Mills Hotel. Forty cents for a room, eighty cents for a suite. The best-dressed man is the first one up in the morning. I'm not advertising these places, folks, I'm just quoting the facts. Now, on these streets, where you see those empty lots there used to be a shanty-town, dwelling places constructed out of wooden boxes and gasoline cans by the unemployed.

WINTHROP

What became of them?

THE GUIDE

The police cleared them out. They made a bad impression on out-of-town folks driving up from the Holland Tunnel. We are now on the lower East Side—the melting pot of humanity. This here is New York's tenement district, and don't forget, folks, that New York has the cream of the world's slums. Five hundred thousand people residing in this district, twenty-seven nationalities. New York has two million Jews, one million seventy thousand Italians, six hundred and thirteen thousand Irish, one hundred and fifteen thousand Hungarians, two hundred and forty Hindus, one hundred and thirty-six Icelanders, each equipped with his own Frigidaire. Note that Jewish reading on your right. That's the Jewish Theayter. Observe the clotheslines, the flags of all nations. Station B.V.D. is on the air to-night. Forty percent of the inhabitants are on home re-lief. Thirty-two percent have spots on their lungs. You know what I mean, folks, T.B.

WINTHROP

Shameful!

THE GUIDE

You said it.

THE FIRST SOUTHERN GIRL

Did you ever smell a worse smell in your life?

THE SECOND SOUTHERN GIRL

No, I honestly never did.

THE GUIDE

We are now on the Bowery, where human wrecks parade in an endless procession. You'll find all sorts here, folks, old men, young men, boys—many of them college graduates or men once famous in the professional world but now ruined by drink or fast living, and swallowed up in this city of derelicts, a city within a city.

(*A group of men, led by a female voice, is heard singing the revivalist hymn, "Brighten the Corner Where You Are."*)

The Bowery, one street two miles long, lined on both sides with flophouses. This building is the famous Bowery Mission. Every night a hundred and fifty men go through that door. When they have money, they have friends; but when they are broke, nobody wants them. They are ashamed to go back to their home towns—they don't want the folks to say, "There goes a boy who couldn't make good."

(JOHN *has listened to this with intense interest.*)

This is Chinatown, folks, queer, weird and fascinating. You are going to see conditions here that you never thought existed. On your right is a beautiful Chinese temple. You must remember that the Chinese do not worship as we do. They just enter the temple and pray to their god, Confucius. Inside the temple you can rub the stomach of the famous Laughing Buddha and see the altar where Lillian Gish lay when filming the movie called *Broken Blossoms*. Now, across the street, you will see the famous Chatham Club, run by Nigger Mike, where Irving Berlin sang for seven years as a singing waiter. In this district, there are always four or five men found dead every morning. They drink that wood alcohol. The police pick up the bodies and take them to the Morgue, where they are kept on ice for ten days. On your left, the world-famous Brooklyn Bridge from which Steve Brodie did his celebrated jump. Built in 1883, 1595 feet long. $100 down and $2 a week buys the Brooklyn Bridge. This is the Fulton Fish Market where Mary Garden used to come to get ideas for her perfumes, and in the little house on the corner Al Smith was born. But he didn't stay there and today he's a multi-millionaire. You know, folks, New York is funny. At the tail end of the Bowery, the financial section begins. This is Wall Street, the deadline for crooks. On the right, corner Broad and Wall, is the Sub-Treasury where George Washington, first president of the United States, took the oath of office. Some say the seat of the government has never moved away from this point. That little park is Bowling Green, scene of the purchase of New York, then called New Amsterdam, by the Dutch. They paid the Indians twenty-four dollars and a keg of rum, cheap at half the price. A few weeks ago a descendant of one of those Indians came to New York, stopped at the Waldorf-Astoria, and had to pay twenty-four dollars for a rum collins. This is the farthest south we can go, folks. Out there is the bay and the Atlantic Ocean, and on an island in the river is the little lady herself, Miss Liberty. Forty-one men can stand in her head and she don't even get a headache. We are now going along the Hudson River, a hundred and fifty miles long and ending at Albany. We are now going to proceed along the express highway. Here we go uphill. We'd appreciate it, folks, if you'll all lean forward to help us up the grade.

(*There is general laughter, as several of the* WOMEN
PASSENGERS *comply.*)

Now you get a good view of the beautiful Hudson. If
you want to see the Hudson and the Palisades, folks, try
our night boat ride. Dine and dance for the price of one
dollar. Take it from me, folks, there's something about
the Hudson at 1 A.M. in the morning. Oh, boy! Those big
piers are where the ocean liners dock. Just ahead, you'll
see the *Normandie,* biggest liner in the world, five city
blocks long, carries two thousand passengers, not counting
stowaways. She's hinged in the middle, so she can go around
corners. We are now entering Harlem, a city within a
city, where four hundred and forty thousand Negroes live,
work and play—Harlem, the Montmartre of Manhattan,
where swing was born, the home of jazz, where witch-
craft and voodoo still flourish. On your left, the heaven
of Father Divine, who is God to thousands of Negroes
and whites. Peace, brother! It's truly wonderful! We now
stop and visit one of Harlem's most beautiful ballrooms,
where we hear Chubby Williams' famous swing band and
see the Negro in his own native environment.

(*Swing music is heard and spotlights illuminate the
stage right and left. The* PASSENGERS *crane their necks
from side to side, as several* NEGRO COUPLES *appear, dancing in a wild and exaggerated manner.*)

Harlem has the highest disease rate, the highest crime
rate, the highest death rate in all New York. But, in
spite of it all, the Negro never loses his native gaiety and
happiness.

THE FIRST SOUTHERN GIRL

(*As a* NEGRO *appears, dancing with a* WHITE WOMAN)

Well, I declare! They sure wouldn't stand for that down in No'th Ca'lina.

THE SECOND SOUTHERN GIRL

No, they sure wouldn't.

(*The* COUPLES *dance off and the lights go out.*)

THE GUIDE

We're on the home stretch now, folks, and on the way back we give you a glimpse of the Great White Way—Broadway—the heart of the world, where three and one-half million lights turn night into day, where every day in the year reputations are made and hearts are broken. Broadway, the street of song and merry-making, the Mecca of tourists from every city and state in the union and every civilized country in the world. Note the Chevrolet sign, the Coca-Cola sign, the Wrigley sign. Note the Strand Theayter, the Capitol Theayter, the Paramount Theayter, the Cotton Club, the Hotel Astor. And so we return you to Times Square, which brings to an end this fascinating tour. And now, as Ethel Barrymore used to finish up, that's all there is, there isn't any more.

(*The lights fade out.*)

Curtain

Scene 3

The private office of LAWRENCE ORMONT. ORMONT *is a slight, dark, sharp-featured man, in his late thirties. At the rise of the curtain, he is seated at his desk, engaged in a telephone conversation. The desk is piled high with play-scripts. At the left, is the door to the outer office.*

ORMONT

Hello, Grace—Well, have you found me a man to play opposite Dorothy Clark?—I thought you were supposed to be a casting-agent. Or am I wrong again?—You don't tell me! Equity has ten thousand members and you can't find me an actor—Who? Darling, it's obvious that I haven't made myself clear. It's an actor I'm looking for, not a dental exhibit—Yes, I know exactly what I want. I want a young George Arliss, with sex appeal—Well, if I knew where to find him, I wouldn't be spending a nickel to talk to you—All right. But I don't think your best is very good—Good-by, dear.

(He hangs up, then immediately picks up the receiver again.)

Are there a lot of hams waiting out there? Well, shoot them in.

(He lights a cigarette. The door opens and a tall, smart-looking GIRL *enters, strides to the middle of the room and begins talking immediately.)*

THE GIRL

Martha Johnson. Two years on the coast with Duffy. Three

seasons in summer stock, playing ingenues and second business. Maisie in the road company of *Heads I Win*. Radio. Last season, general understudy in *Hot Money*. The season before that, three flops. I want a chance to act. I know I'm tall, but I can't do anything about that. Do I look like anything?

> ORMONT

(Without expression)

No.

> THE GIRL

(Briskly)

Thank you!

(She turns and strides out. Almost immediately, a very FRAGILE YOUNG MAN *flounces in.)*

> ORMONT

(The moment he sees him)

Definitely not.

> THE YOUNG MAN

(Stopping dead)

Sorry!

(He flounces out. The door opens again and JOHN *enters, carrying a large manila envelope.)*

> JOHN

Hello, Mr. Ormont.

(Extending his hand)

I'm glad to see you again.

> ORMONT

I wish I could say the same. Who are you?

> JOHN

John Thompson. I didn't expect you to remember me.

ORMONT

What have you done?

JOHN

Nothing to speak of, in the way of acting, if that's what you mean. I'm not an actor.

ORMONT

The first one I've ever heard admit it.

(*Looking at* JOHN's *envelope*)

You wouldn't be a playwright?

JOHN

Well, I hope to convince you that I am.

ORMONT

Hallelujah! I knew there must be one somewhere.

(*Rising*)

Drop in again. I'm seldom here.

JOHN

I know that. That's why I'm going to make the most of this opportunity. I met you out at the University of Iowa, two years ago, when you came out to see our production of *The Land I Love*.

ORMONT

Oh yes, that epic of the cow pasture. I have bitter memories of the occasion. My boy, you're deluding yourself. You are *not* a playwright.

JOHN

Oh, I didn't write that play. I only stage-managed it. But you told me that if I ever came to New York, you'd be glad to see me.

ORMONT

But how was I to suspect that you had any intention of coming to New York?

JOHN

Oh, there never was any doubt about that. It was just a
question of scraping together enough money to get me
here. Well, this spring, I won the annual two hundred
dollar prize for the best student play. So here I am.

ORMONT

That's obvious. And you're giving me the first chance
at the great American drama. I'm touched.

JOHN

Well, I'm not sure it's as good as all that.

ORMONT

No false modesty, Thompson. That'll never get you anywhere. What is this opus? Another one of those chicken-
run sagas?

JOHN

It's called *Red Cloud* and it's about the people who live
in the dust bowl.

ORMONT

Just what McBride's customers are waiting for. A pro-
letarian document, no doubt. The drought, it appears, is
all the fault of the capitalist system. Morgan's yacht rides
in fifty fathoms of water, and in Kansas not a drop falls.
On to the barricades, comrades!

JOHN

No, it's not like that, at all. There's nothing red about
it except the title.

ORMONT

What? No social significance? What the hell are you, an
escapist?

JOHN

Well, I'm a fugitive from a cornfield, if that's what you

mean. Anyhow, this is just a play about the kind of people
I know and grew up with—good, plain, hard-working Middle-Western farm people, who suddenly find themselves
caught up in something they don't understand and can't do
anything about. That's a situation that ought to be mighty
interesting to a lot of folks, because it's a fix that an awful
lot of them are in, right this very minute—unless the
newspapers are just kidding.

ORMONT

Listen, Thompson, I was majoring in sociology at Yale,
before you were housebroke. What's more, I'm a Middle-
Western boy, myself—the black sheep of one of the worst
families in Evansville, Indiana. So don't try to tell me
what goes on. What you want to do is make up your mind
whether you want to be a playwright or an editor of the
New Republic.

JOHN

I made up my mind about that long ago—even before I
began reading the *New Republic.* I've come here not only
to sell my play, but to learn all I can about the professional theater. The theatrical pickings are pretty lean back
where I come from. Now and then, we get a road company
in Des Moines, but that's about all. And you'd be surprised
how many folks out there are theater-hungry. It seems to
me that—

ORMONT

(Breaking in)
Some day, when I retire from show business, let's get together and discuss the drama. Meanwhile, if you'll excuse
me, I'll go back to casting this little penthouse number
I've got in the works now. *Long Island Honeymoon!*

What a title! What a play! As unnecessary a manuscript as I've ever read.

JOHN

Then why does a great producer like you put it on? Or is that an impertinent question?

ORMONT

I like impertinence. It makes me feel less alone in the world. I'll tell you why I'm putting it on. Because a little exhibitionistic bitch, whose grandfather stole half the country's natural resources, is itching to put on grease paint. Any other questions?—impertinent or pertinent, it doesn't matter which. I'm catholic in my tastes.

JOHN

Yes, I have one very pertinent one. How soon will you read my play?

ORMONT

Can you give me twenty-four hours?

JOHN

Could you read it in a week? I don't want to submit it to anybody else, as long as there's a chance of your doing it.

ORMONT

I appreciate that, Thompson. Bernard Shaw could take lessons in manners from you. Tell me, are there any snappy hayloft scenes in this play?

JOHN

Well, there's one situation in it that may be a little hard to get past the Hays organization.

ORMONT

That's encouraging. Next to a good penthouse, give me a good hayloft. I had begun to visualize it as all fine, choking dust and the bleaching skeletons of large domestic animals.

Put it on the pile there. Carefully, so it doesn't topple over. I'm going to read them over the weekend. Or I may not. You never know with me.

JOHN

I hope you will. And there's one thing more I'm going to ask of you, Mr. Ormont.

ORMONT

Anything, Thompson. Anything but my daughter's hand. She's only twelve—too young for marriage.

JOHN

Then I guess I'd better wait till she grows up. Anyhow, all my prospects are in that envelope, so I may not be much of a catch right now. How about giving me a job, Mr. Ormont? I know I could handle an assistant stage managership and some understudies or anything at all— secretary, errand boy, bouncer. I worked my way through high school and college and I've done just about everything —farm hand, waiter, garage mechanic, deputy sheriff—

ORMONT

(*Edging him toward the door*)

Well, I don't need any farm hands or deputy sheriffs right now. What I am looking for is a young George Arliss with sex appeal.

JOHN

Gosh, you would mention the one thing I'm not quite right for. But keep me in mind, will you?

(*Shaking hands*)

Good-by, Mr. Ormont. I'll be back in a week to find out what you think of the play.

ORMONT

You won't forget?

JOHN

(*Laughing*)　I'll try not to.

(*He exits. The telephone rings and* ORMONT *answers it.*)

ORMONT

Yes—Who?—I'm not in—Listen, dummkopf, haven't I ex-
plained to you that I'm never in?—How many times do I
have to tell you that I'm not on speaking terms with any
of my friends—All right, put him on—Hello, Eddie—Well,
Eddie, since you ask me, I'm not going to do anything
about it—No, I can't pay you a little something on account
—Listen, Eddie, darling, I haven't got a hundred dollars.
I haven't got ten dollars. I haven't got a dime. I'm bum-
ming cigarettes from the elevator boy. And if I ever lost
those telephone numbers, I'd be sleeping in the Park—All
right, sue me! Send me to Atlanta! Crucify me!

(*He bangs down the receiver. The door opens and*
HEINZ KALTBART, *a thin, pale, shabbily dressed man enters, timidly.*)

KALTBART

How do you do, Mr. Ormont?

(*He speaks with a heavy Continental accent.*)

ORMONT

Nothing.

KALTBART

Excuse me, Mr. Ormont, if you could give me only two
minutes. My name is Heinz Kaltbart and I am—

ORMONT

Yes, I know. You were a prize pupil of Max Reinhardt's,
and you acted for eighteen years in the Burgtheater of
Vienna and the Grosses Schauspeilhaus of Berlin and the
Ratskeller of Pilsen. You've played everything from King

Lear to premature babies. You speak German, French,
Italian, Ukranian and Esperanto. You can paint scenery,
walk the tightrope and you have a marvelous recipe for
bouillabaisse.

KALTBART

Not quite so much as that, Mr. Ormont. But I have had
many years' experience, I am a good actor, I—

ORMONT

Nothing, I tell you.

KALTBART

Even the smallest part. Anything. In the play you are
producing, there is perhaps—

ORMONT

The play I am producing is called *Long Island Honeymoon* and deals with the cocktail set—a lot of social twirps,
with strong Southampton accents.

KALTBART

Yes, I know my English is not yet perfect. I study hard
but for us the pronunciation is difficult. But if you could
only give me something. An assistant to the stage manager.
Or an usher. Only to work in the theater again. Now I am
selling newspapers in the cafés.

ORMONT

(*Pacing the office*)

Why do you come to me? Why in hell does every European refugee take a taxi direct from the pier to my office?
When was I elected Führer of the Chosen People?

KALTBART

It is only that we must find work. Thank you for being
so kind as to see me, Mr. Ormont.

(*He goes toward the door.*)

ORMONT

Here, wait a minute!

(*He takes out his wallet.*)

Here's twenty dollars for you. Fifteen will buy you a suit and five a pair of shoes. The sales tax you'll have to dig up, yourself.

KALTBART

No, no, I cannot take money!

ORMONT

What do you mean, you cannot take money? Pride goes before a fall, not after it. Go on, put it in your pocket.

KALTBART

How can I thank you, Mr. Ormont?

ORMONT

Don't thank me. I'm not doing this for you. I'm doing it to salve my own conscience, because I'm a yellow, callous heel that wastes his time and his talents catering to the tastes of morons, instead of getting out and fighting injustice and persecution.

(*The telephone rings and he waves* KALTBART *away.*)

All right! Leave your address with the girl on the way out.

KALTBART

Thank you, Mr. Ormont.

(*He exits.*)

ORMONT

(*At the telephone*)

Well?—Dorothy Clark! Oh, tell her—! All right, shoot her right in.

(*He hangs up. The door opens and* DOROTHY CLARK *enters, a pretty girl of twenty-five, very smartly dressed. She carries a playscript.*)

DOROTHY

Hello, Larry.

ORMONT

(*Hurrying forward to greet her*)

Hello, Dot. God, you look more wonderful every time I see you. How in hell do you do it? Sit down.

DOROTHY

Well, I've only got a minute. I just popped in to say hello, on my way to the hairdresser's.

(*She sits beside the desk.*)

Honestly, Larry, I'm so excited about this production, I just can't talk about anything else. Every time I think of that opening night, I get goose-bumps all over me.

ORMONT

Well, that's the theater. Once it gets you, it gets you. We're all a little mad, we theater-addicts, but it's a kind of divine madness, don't you think?

DOROTHY

Yes, that's exactly how I feel. You know, the more I think about the title, the better I like it—*Long Island Honeymoon!*

ORMONT

It says something.

DOROTHY

That's what I mean. I go around hugging this script like crazy. I just don't seem able to put it down. I'm going to read it again, while I'm having my hair done. It *is* good, isn't it?

ORMONT

Well, Dot, I get to read a lot of scripts, for my sins, but

I've never read a shrewder one than that. It's the sheer economy of the thing that fascinates me.

DOROTHY

And you do think it will go, don't you?

ORMONT

Well, if you want me to be perfectly honest with you, I don't see how it can miss.

DOROTHY

Oh, I hope so! I had dinner with Tommy Bellows last night, and he says I'm an awful fool to put money into a play. He thinks I ought to have my head examined.

ORMONT

Lawyers! What is a lawyer? A eunuch who spends the first thirty years of his life training himself to think in terms of five percent. A parasite who has neither the agility of the flea nor the curiosity of the louse.

DOROTHY

Well, I told him that after all it's my own money and if I feel like backing a show it's no business of his.

ORMONT

(*Patting her hand*)

I like you. Beauty, wit and guts. I've never encountered it before.

DOROTHY

Larry, you're sweet! And you do think I'm going to be good, don't you? There'll be an awful lot of people out there just sitting back and waiting for me to make a fool of myself. And you know what the newspapers are like. Just because I have money, they think they can say anything they like about me.

ORMONT

Yes, I know, the capitalist press. Do you want the un-varnished truth?

DOROTHY

Yes, I certainly do.

ORMONT

I knew you would. You've got character. Well, here it is. Sitting here at this desk, I'd say you have more natural talent for the stage than any girl I've seen in two years.

DOROTHY

Well, I'm glad you really think so. Because if you didn't know, who would?

ORMONT

Well, I didn't like to say that.

DOROTHY

I've got to run, now. Why don't we have lunch? I want to talk to you about the script. I really think it would help the play, if my scene with Toddles in the third act could be built up a little.

ORMONT

The very thing I've been wanting to suggest to you.

DOROTHY

Oh, I'm so glad you agree with me! It's really an inspiration to work with a person like you, Larry.

ORMONT

Well, you bring out the best in me—and that's not bad.

DOROTHY

I should say not! The Colony at two?

ORMONT

I'll be there at one-fifty-five. A slight, dapper man, in a business suit.

(He kisses her hand.)

You're lovely!

DOROTHY

Adios!
(She exits. ORMONT shakes his head, sighs and goes toward his desk, as the door opens and MARY enters.)

MARY

Good morning, Mr. Ormont.

ORMONT

Take your hat off. Pull up your skirts. What's your name?

MARY

Mary Ward.

ORMONT

Very good for lights.

MARY

Yes, that's what I think, too.

ORMONT

For my own good, don't yes me. My head is easily turned. And what's your history? A blank, no doubt.

MARY

Almost, but not quite. Do you mind if I sit down?

ORMONT

I didn't dare hope you would. Do you find that chair comfortable?

MARY

Yes, very. And I consider myself very lucky to be sitting in it and talking to you. I didn't expect to get in.

ORMONT

I'm a masochist.

MARY

Do you want to know what I've done?

ORMONT

No. But tell me, anyhow.

MARY

Well, to begin at the very beginning, I've been mad about the stage ever since I was about five—

ORMONT

Let's get down to modern times. I'm catching a midnight train.

MARY

Well, when I was in high school—

ORMONT

You joined the Dramatic Society and you played Rosalind and Peter Pan and Roxanne in *Cyrano de Bergerac*.

MARY

How did you know that?

ORMONT

I'm psychic.

MARY

I suppose you hear the same story twenty times a day.

ORMONT

Forty. Now tell me about the summer stock.

MARY

Oh dear! You take the words right out of a poor girl's mouth. It's not fair!

ORMONT

Did you ever support Mrs. Fiske?

MARY

Not that I remember. Who is Mrs. Fiske?

ORMONT

That's an intelligent question. Now I'll ask you one. What makes you think you can act?

MARY

Well, I just know I can. And that isn't just conceit either. I haven't done anything that counts on Broadway, I know that. But I've played a lot of different kinds of parts and I know that I've played some of them very well. If you'll just give me a chance, I'm sure I can convince you that I'm an actress. And being able to watch a wonderful director like you would mean all the world to me, right now. So be nice, Mr. Ormont, and give me a walk-on or an understudy or anything. Just a chance to get started—that's all I ask.

ORMONT

The place for you to get started for, is back to Vermont.

MARY

New Hampshire's where I come from.

ORMONT

All right, I'll settle for New Hampshire.

MARY

But why? I've only just got here. And I came away because I want to be an actress and all I could ever be back home is a schoolteacher.

ORMONT

A noble calling. The profession of Socrates and Woodrow Wilson.

MARY

Yes, I suppose so; but I'd rather be Helen Hayes than President. There's no use trying to discourage me, Mr. Ormont. I've never wanted to do anything but be an actress. Only when you're a country doctor's daughter, you have to think about making a living, and that's why I went in for teaching. Then, last spring, my grandmother died and left me five hundred dollars. So here I am and here I'm going to stay.

ORMONT

At this moment, ninety-five thousand girls, all with the same idea—if you can call it an idea—are converging upon New York from the forty-eight states of the Union, Alaska, Puerto Rico, Guam and the Virgin Islands—well, maybe not the Virgin Islands. It's all that's keeping the railroads from bankruptcy. Tomorrow, they'll all be in this office.

MARY

Then I *was* lucky to get in today.

ORMONT

Go home, I tell you. Broadway is paved with the little white psyches of renegade schoolteachers.

MARY

I'll never go home. Except to show the folks in Laconia my notices.

(*She rises.*)

So don't think you've seen the last of me, Mr. Ormont. I'm going to haunt your doorstep until you at least give me a chance to read for you. Thanks, anyhow, for listening to me. I'll be seeing you again.

(*She starts to go.*)

ORMONT

(*As she reaches the door*)

Wait a minute!

(MARY *turns.*)

Come in, tomorrow.

MARY

(*Eagerly*)

Do you really mean it?

ORMONT

Oh, I wouldn't go that far.

MARY

What time?

ORMONT

Any time. I probably won't be here.

MARY

I'll come when the office opens and wait all day.

ORMONT

That's right, bring your lunch. And an extra sandwich for me.

(*The telephone rings, and he picks up the receiver.*)

MARY

Thank you, Mr. Ormont!

(*She exits, exultantly.*)

ORMONT

Yes?—All right—Hello, beautiful—Oh, I'm looking my loveliest. And you?—You sound unclothed and hanging over a little—Did we have fun, last night?—What do you say we have fun tonight?—The Merry-Go-Round at seven?—I'm as good as there, honeysuckle.

(*While he is talking, the*

Curtain Falls

Scene 4

A longitudinal section of a subway car of the type used on the B. M. T. system. We see only the right-hand side of the car, that is to say, the side which adjoins the station platforms. In the center, is one of the entrance doors. On either side of the door, against the wall of the car, is a seat accommodating two persons. To the right and left are two seats, at right angles to the wall of the car. At the rise of the curtain, the train is moving and we hear the roar of its motion and see through the windows, the rhythmic flicker of the fixed lights in the tube. All the seats are occupied and there are eight or ten PASSENGERS standing. MRS. LEVY is seated in the cross-seat, just to the left of the doorway. Among the standees, are FREDERIC WINTHROP and KATHERINE WINTHROP HOLMES, a well-dressed, attractive young woman. There is a miscellany of other PASSENGERS, including many of the characters in the play. Among them is the sailor DIXIE BUSHBY, who sits near the door. Most of the PASSENGERS are reading books or newspapers, one or two are dozing. After a few moments, the flicker of lights becomes less staccato, as the train slows down, on its approach to a station.

MRS. LEVY

(Nervously to the man beside her)

Excuse me, do I get off here to go to the Aquarium?

THE MAN

Why, I really couldn't tell you. I'm a stranger here, myself.

ANOTHER PASSENGER

No, you've got a long ways to go yet. Get off at Bowling Green.

MRS. LEVY

Thank you.

(*As the train stops, several of the* PASSENGERS *get off, as* STANDEES *scramble for the vacated seats.* OTHERS *enter from station platform. As the door starts to close, a* MAN *looks up from his newspaper, sees that it is his station and makes a dash for the door, colliding with* KATHERINE. *He makes no apology, but rushes out through the closing door. The train starts to move again.*)

KATHERINE

Oh, this is really awful! I don't see why we couldn't have taken a taxi.

WINTHROP

Can't I make you understand that I've given up all these luxuries that the workers can't afford?

KATHERINE

Well, I suppose I'm very dense about the whole thing; but I really don't see how you help raise the standards of the laboring class by lowering your own.

WINTHROP

The point is that I have too much self-respect to go on indulging myself, while millions of people are without the bare necessities of life.

KATHERINE

Your self-respect doesn't seem to prevent you from living on inherited money.

WINTHROP

That's damned unfair! I only use a small part of my income for myself. The rest I give to the movement.

KATHERINE

Well, you've managed to make us all pretty unhappy, I don't mind telling you. If this is what four years of Harvard does for boys, I hope to heaven no child of mine ever goes there.

WINTHROP

Oh, don't malign poor old Harvard. I assure you it's still safe and respectable enough even for your children.

KATHERINE

Well, what's brought all this about then? Don't tell me it's your great sympathy for people who are badly off that has suddenly turned you into a red. You're just about as selfish as anybody can be.

WINTHROP

Unselfishness doesn't flourish in the environment in which you and I grew up. Anyhow, this isn't a matter of feeling sorry for individuals. You see everything in personal and romantic terms. Actually, Marxism is an exact science, governed by immutable laws, like physics or mathematics. But you're so walled in by prejudice that you're incapable even of listening.

KATHERINE

If it's prejudiced to believe that a boy shouldn't deliberately throw away his position in the world and his whole future and make everybody who cares for him unhappy, then I'm glad to admit that I am prejudiced.

WINTHROP

Position and money! You can't think beyond that, can

you? Well, it happens that I don't want a future as a mine-owner. I don't want to live by exploiting the lives and the labor of others. I prefer to help build a world in which there is a decent future for everybody.

(*Breaking off as the train comes to a stop again*)
We get off here.

KATHERINE

(*As they exit*)
Well, thank goodness for that! I've never been so jostled and jolted in my life. And the air in here—! I don't believe you have any convictions about it, at all. It's just a lot of talk.

(*Again there is general movement. A* PASSENGER *in the seat at the left gets off as* ORMONT *and* CLIFTON ROSS, *the artist, enter from the car platform.* ROSS *takes the vacant seat and* ORMONT *stands beside him. The train starts again.*)

ROSS

What I don't understand is how you ever could have believed that that show had a Chinaman's chance.

ORMONT

I didn't.

ROSS

If you had the brains of a grasshopper, you'd have known that that rookie from the Junior League could never get to first base.

ORMONT

I did.

ROSS

Then why in hell did you do it?

ORMONT

Item, a director's salary. Item, a manager's salary. Item, office overhead. Item, some kick-backs from the petits bourgeois who made the clothes and the furniture.

ROSS

And that's what you did it for?

ORMONT

That's right. I'm a little punk of a chiseler. Maybe we'll sell the picture rights. After all, they bought *Gone With The Wind*.

ROSS

You're slipping, Larry. A couple more like that and you'll be through as a producer.

ORMONT

I like you, Cliff. A blunt, honest fellow. Been tearing the wings off any flies, lately?

ROSS

Why don't you try producing a good play?

ORMONT

Why don't you write me one, Cliff?

ROSS

Well, I've never written a line in my life, but—

ORMONT

I know. But you wouldn't live here if they gave you the place. Who do you think will win the Yale-Harvard game? I'm betting on Joe Louis.

ROSS

What about those costume designs I made?

ORMONT

That's a very interesting question.

Ross

You may recall that a thousand dollars was to change hands.

Ormont

They're worth at least twice that.

Ross

I know they are. But what about it?

Ormont

Do you want the coat off my back?

Ross

It wouldn't fit me.

(*As the train comes to a stop*)

I want a thousand dollars.

Ormont

(*As they exit*)

What are you trying to do—crucify me?

(*There is a general movement, as some* Passengers *exit and others enter.* John *enters at the right and takes one of the cross-seats near the door. He turns, recognizes the* Man *who is sitting back-to-back to him and taps his shoulder.*)

John

Excuse me, but aren't you Martin Blake?

Blake

(*Looking up in surprise*)

Yes, that's right.

John

Thompson's my name. I used to watch you play full-back for Iowa.

BLAKE

(*Shaking hands*)

Glad to know you. When were you at Iowa?

JOHN

I only got out a year ago. I always wanted to meet you, but I never thought it would be in a New York subway train.

BLAKE

Well, you'd be surprised how many Iowa men you meet around New York. How are things back there?

JOHN

They haven't changed much. Everybody I know is still trying to keep one jump ahead of the tax collectors—and still hoping that things will be better next year. Haven't you been back since you graduated?

BLAKE

No, I haven't. I wanted to make the fifth reunion of my class, but I just couldn't get away.

JOHN

I've read about you in the *Alumni News*. You seem to be scoring a lot of touchdowns in the insurance field.

BLAKE

Well, being selected for the All-American team doesn't hurt a man a bit in a business way. How long you been in New York?

JOHN

About three months. And having a hell of an exciting time, too. There's something terrifically dynamic about it all—something that gets you going and keeps you going.

BLAKE

Well, that wears off, after a while. You planning to settle here?

JOHN

Yes, I am. At least I think I am. I got a letter from my brother yesterday, asking me to come back. He's just taken over the Chevrolet agency in Waterloo and he wants me to go in with him.

BLAKE

Sounds pretty good. If you ask me, a lot of fellows would do a whole heap better staying right in their own communities, where they've got good connections, instead of trying to crash through this New York formation.

JOHN

The trouble is I'm not interested in selling Chevrolets. I wouldn't even be interested in selling Cadillacs.

BLAKE

What *is* your line?

JOHN

I'm trying to write plays. Or, I should say, to sell the ones I've written. But all I've managed to do so far is establish one good connection. You've heard of Lawrence Ormont, the theatrical producer, haven't you?

BLAKE

No. I don't follow the theater much.

JOHN

Well, Ormont is about the best of the New York producers. He's had a play of mine for over two months now. That either means that he's considering it seriously—or that he just hasn't read it, at all.

BLAKE

I wonder how much insurance protection a fellow like that carries. What did you say his name is?

JOHN

Lawrence Ormont. But I don't think you'll find him a very good prospect. I don't believe he has any money.

BLAKE

I thought you said he's the best in the business.

JOHN

Yes, but it's the theatrical business. You don't happen to know where I could get a job, do you?

BLAKE

No, I can't say that I do. From all I hear, jobs are pretty scarce, these days.

JOHN

Yes, I've found that out. One of the things that I haven't come across yet in New York is a door mat with "Welcome" written on it. I'd feel a little better about all this, if I knew a few congenial folks that I could sit around and talk to. But so far my acquaintance is pretty strictly limited to office boys and elevator operators.

BLAKE

(*Stifling a yawn*)

Oh, sure, it takes time to get acquainted.

JOHN

(*Rising as the train slows down*)

I get off here. It's a fine experience, Mr. Blake, to meet one of your boyhood heroes.

BLAKE

Well, thanks; I'm always glad to run into anybody from good, old Iowa.

(JOHN *makes a dash for the door, which is beginning to close, brushing against* MARY, *who is just entering from the station platform.* MARY, *unable to find a seat, stands at one of the poles, near* MRS. LEVY, *but with her newspaper held before her face. A* LITTLE MAN *with a portable radio takes the seat vacated by* JOHN *and begins to doze off.*)

MRS. LEVY

(*Tugging at* MARY's *newspaper*)

Good morning. I'm glad to see you again.

MARY

(*Uncertainly*)

Oh, how do you do?

MRS. LEVY

I guess maybe you don't remember me. I'm Mrs. Levy. We sat on the same seat in the sightseeing bus.

MARY

Why, of course we did! It's awfully nice to see you again. Are you getting used to New York?

MRS. LEVY

In time you get used to everything. And now I'm beginning to know my way around, a little. And how do you like it here?

MARY

Oh, I think it's just too marvelous!

MRS. LEVY

Yes, for young people, it must be wonderful. But for an old lady—well, sometimes it's a little too much. In Elmira I had my own little house and my friends—but here, it's different.

MARY

Yes, I know just what you mean. It takes such a long time to get acquainted with people here! But you have your family, haven't you?

MRS. LEVY

Oh yes, of course! But, you know the way it is. Young people are always busy. But I can't complain. I read books from the circulating library, and right across the street is a movie theater. Twice a week they have different pictures. And, when the weather's good, I go sightseeing. Now I'm going to the Aquarium. I suppose you were there already?

MARY

No, I've never been. I'm dying to go. And to the Bronx Zoo, too.

MRS. LEVY

Last week, I went to the Bronx Zoo. It's very pretty, the way they have it fixed up. And the animals are wonderful —lions and elephants and I don't know what. And such beautiful birds. So, now I thought I'll go and see the Aquarium, too. Fishes I'm not so crazy about; but it helps pass the time. But how about you? Are you on the stage now?

MARY

Why, no, I'm not. I did have a part in a play called *Long Island Honeymoon* but it only lasted two weeks. So, I'll have to find some other kind of work until another part comes along. That's where I'm going right now—to look for a job.

(*Meanwhile,* THE LITTLE MAN, *with the portable radio on his lap, has fallen sound asleep.* DIXIE BUSHBY *reaches over and turns on the radio. The* MAN *awakes with a start and the* OTHER PASSENGERS *turn to look, as the radio blares forth.*)

THE RADIO

You are probably suffering from skin starvation. Why not treat your skin to a square meal tonight with Calloway's Compound Cream, the new beauty aid that thousands of women are learning to use?

(*In the middle of this, the*

Curtain Falls

ACT TWO

Scene 5

The Studio Apartment of CLIFTON ROSS. *A large, rather untidy, but comfortable room. At the back, large windows and a sloping skylight afford a north light. The entrance door is at the left and the bedroom door is at the right.*
ROSS, *in his shirt sleeves, is at a draughting table, making a water-color drawing of* MARY, *who stands on a platform, wearing a bathing suit, her arms held in the pose of a swimmer poised for a dive.*

ROSS

Getting tired?

MARY

No, it's all right.

ROSS

About three minutes more and then we'll take a rest.

MARY

What's it going to be—another cigarette ad?

ROSS

No. Breakfast food, this time. The same idea, though. The high-powered psychologists who work for the advertising agencies have discovered that the public doesn't give a damn about the difference between one brand of canned soup and another—assuming that there is any difference. But if you can associate your product with a pretty girl, preferably half-dressed, you suggest to the customer that when he buys the tooth paste, he somehow gets the girl, too.

MARY

Why, I never thought of that! And I'm not sure that I like it, either.

ROSS

Why?

MARY

Well—I don't know. But I just don't.

ROSS

It makes you feel self-conscious?

MARY

Well, a little, I guess.

ROSS

(*Going to her and adjusting her head*)

What did you think was the purpose of this absence of costume? Did you think you were giving a scientific demonstration of the dietetic values of Yummie-Yums?

MARY

I guess I didn't think about it. I've just been concentrating on the three dollars an hour. I wish you hadn't brought it up.

ROSS

Sorry. But my models are usually somewhat less sensitive.

(*The telephone rings and he tickles her under the arm.*)

All right—relax!

MARY

(*Squirming*)

Don't!

(*She lowers her arms, steps off the platform, and lights a cigarette, as* Ross *answers the phone.*)

ROSS

Hello— Yes— Oh hello, Miss Clark— Yes, I'm just in the

middle of a little allegorical masterpiece called The
Triumph of Virtue over Commercialism— Never mind,
I'll explain some other time— Well, I'm sorry to say, I've
decided not to do it— I don't think I'd do a very good
job— That's very charming of you, but I know better.
Look, could I talk you into having dinner with me tomorrow night?—Swell. Suppose I pick you up at seven-
ish?—Done and done. Good-by.

(*He hangs up.*)

MARY

Are we going on?

ROSS

There's no hurry. I'll only need a half-hour or so more.
How about a drink?

MARY

No, thank you! I'm still aware of that cocktail for lunch.

ROSS

Well, I'm having some brandy. Sure you won't join me?

MARY

Positive. I must say I didn't care for that remark about
the triumph of virtue.

ROSS

You don't like your virtue.

MARY

I don't like the word. It has an awful Sunday-School
sound about it. It makes me feel like a character in *Little
Women*.

ROSS

(*Patting her cheek*)

Be good, sweet maid, and let who will, be clever. Not that
you're not clever, too.

MARY

Well, I'm glad you added that! I think I'll put on my coat.

ROSS

It's at least seventy-five in here. Modesty?

MARY

Well, I'm not exactly used to sitting around like this—not indoors, anyhow.

ROSS

Wait a minute and I'll get you something better. I adore you!

(*He hobbles off to the bedroom. MARY walks about, a little uneasily. In a moment or two, Ross returns with a gaily striped silk robe.*)

ROSS

Try this.

MARY

Oh, how lovely!

ROSS

(*Helping her into it*)

Like it?

MARY

Why, I never saw anything so beautiful! The colors! And what a gorgeous fabric!

ROSS

Yes, it's a good one. You look very nice in it!

MARY

Well, who wouldn't? Where does it come from?

ROSS

Bokhara. That's down in Central Asia. But I picked it up in a junk shop in Tiflis.

MARY

You've been just about everywhere, haven't you?

ROSS

Well, I like to move around.

MARY

What are you smiling at?

ROSS

You.

MARY

I wish you wouldn't.

ROSS

All right, I'll glower.

MARY

No, that's not necessary, either. Do you mind if I look at the picture?

ROSS

(Laughing)

Of course not! It's intended for a wide audience.

MARY

Well, some artists don't like you to see what they're doing until it's all finished.

(She rises and goes to the draughting table.)

ROSS

This has nothing to do with art. It's what the Germans call *Kunstgewerbe*.

MARY

What does that mean?

ROSS

Well, handicraft, roughly speaking. You don't have to

keep on that bathing cap. It doesn't go well with the rest
of the costume.

(*He starts to take it off.*)

MARY

Oh, don't take it off! It'll take hours to get it on right
again.

Ross

There's lots of time. I like your hair.

MARY

Yes, it must look charming after being under that cap
for an hour.

(*She walks away from the draughting table.*)

You certainly do draw beautifully.

Ross

Oh, I'm a Grade-A draughtsman. Prix de Rome at the
Beaux Arts and all that.

MARY

It must be wonderful to have genius.

Ross

That's not genius, it's talent. As somebody said, genius is
the usual thing, talent the exception.

MARY

I don't understand that.

Ross

Well, never mind. Are you under the impression that I
always take my models to lunch?

MARY

Well, I was wondering a little about that.

Ross

You needn't. Most of them are extremely dull little girls
from Tenth Avenue, with rather dirty feet.

MARY

Well, it's nice to know that cleanliness is one virtue you don't object to. I wish you'd tell me why your drawings have nothing to do with art.

ROSS

I think I was just making a bow to the piddling little half-talents, who justify their own failure by smearing with the scarlet letter of commercialism every artist who is able to earn his living. As a matter of fact, most of the great painters were damned shrewd business men. Some of the greatest works of Titian and Michelangelo were executed to order at so much per square yard. I happen to be a lad who would rather glorify a brassière that emphasizes that all-important dividing line and get five hundred dollars for it, than do a similar arrangement of a couple of apples and eat a salami sandwich at the Automat.

MARY

Well, I think it's too bad that someone like you isn't doing things to hang in museums, instead of for the back covers of magazines.

ROSS

Well, you see, I happen to know that I'm not that good. To paint like Velasquez and be the buddy of kings, or to paint like Cezanne and starve—that's a career. But to be an in-betweener, a fellow who, for a fee, conceals what he sees in a banker's face—no thank you. As a matter of fact, you just heard me refuse to do a portrait of a very rich young rich girl, because I've seen all the great portraits in all the great galleries of the world.

MARY

Do you mind my asking if that was Dorothy Clark?

Ross

Yes, it was. Do you know her?

Mary

Well, slightly. We happened to be in a play together, a few months ago.

Ross

What do you mean a play? Not that mess of tripe that Larry Ormont dished up to an outraged public?

Mary

Yes.

Ross

But wait a minute! I saw that play, God help me, and I haven't the faintest recollection of your being in it.

Mary

There's no earthly reason why you should have. All I did was the tiniest bit in the second act.

Ross

Why have you been keeping this from me?

Mary

Well, I was afraid you wouldn't give me the job if I told you that I'm not a regular model. I'm sorry I lied about it, but I did need the job.

Ross

You're forgiven. Especially since I didn't believe anything you told me.

Mary

Then why did you give me the job?

Ross

I guess I must have liked your looks. I guess I still do. Won't Ormont give you a job in his next show?

MARY

I don't know. I'm not sure that I'd want it.

ROSS

Why? Did he make passes at you?
  (MARY *does not answer.*)
Dear old Larry! Tell me about it.

MARY

I'd rather not talk about it, if you don't mind.
  (*Impulsively*)
I really don't think it's very nice of a man to try to take
advantage of somebody who's working for him, especially
when he knows she needs the job.

ROSS

There's no concealed barb in that observation, is there?

MARY

I guess I'm talking too much. Are we going to go on with
the picture?

ROSS

In a few minutes. I'm going to have another drink first.
You haven't changed your mind?

MARY

No, thanks.

ROSS

  (*Pouring himself a drink*)
So you think I'm taking an unfair advantage of you, do
you?

MARY

I didn't say that.

ROSS

No?

MARY

No. This is entirely different. I didn't have to accept your invitation to lunch.

ROSS

Well, to a thrifty girl, every lunch is that much to the good.

MARY

Now, that's really unkind. You know that wasn't the reason.

ROSS

What was the reason?

MARY

Well—don't make me say it. Because you're clever and a fine artist and an important person.

ROSS

Certainly no more so than Ormont.

MARY

But I don't like him.

ROSS

Am I to consider that a declaration of love?

MARY

You're really making me feel very embarrassed. Can't we talk about something else?

ROSS

Sure. How long have you been in New York?

MARY

About six months.

ROSS

Small town girl?

MARY

Yes.

Ross

And you've never had a lover?

Mary

(*Greatly embarrassed*)
You *do* ask the damnedest questions!

Ross

How old are you?

Mary

Twenty.

Ross

Haven't you any curiosity?

Mary

Yes, of course, I have. Please stop!

Ross

Come over here by me.
(*She does not answer.*)
Don't you want to?

Mary

Yes. But I won't.

Ross

Does my deformity bother you? Is that it?

Mary

No, of course not! How can you say such a thing?

Ross

I just didn't know. Different women react differently to
things like that. Some like deformities—it's one of those
attraction-repulsion things. And sometimes, there's an
appeal to the maternal instinct—

Mary

I don't understand any of what you're talking about. I'm
frightened now. I'm really frightened.

Ross

I didn't mean to upset you. Why should you be afraid
of me?

MARY

I don't know why, but I am. And of myself even more.

Ross

Why?

MARY

Because I'm lonely and confused. Because I don't understand you or myself or what's happening to me.

Ross

All right. Let's get back to work.

MARY

Couldn't we finish it tomorrow? I'd like to get some
shopping done before the stores close.

Ross

No, I promised it for the first thing in the morning. Come
on.

(*He helps her out of the robe and hands her the bathing
cap.*)

MARY

Do I have to put on the cap, too?

Ross

Yes. The head still needs a little work. Here, let me help
you.

MARY

Thanks, I can do it alone!

(*She forces her hair under the tight cap.*)

Do I look all right?

Ross ·

You look lovely.

(*He suddenly clasps her in his arms and kisses her.*
MARY *resists at first, then puts her arms around his
neck. There is a knock at the door.* ROSS *instinctively
loosens his hold on her and she slips away from him.*)

Ross

Never mind that. They'll go away. Mary—

(*He tries to draw her to him. There is another knock
at the door.*)

MARY

You'd better answer it!

(*She frees herself and quickly enters the bedroom.* ROSS
*hesitates, uncertain whether to follow her or not. An-
other knock.*)

ROSS

Come in!

(*The entrance door opens and* JOHN *enters, carrying a
voluminous leather brief case.*)

JOHN

Mr. Ross?

ROSS

Yes. What is it?

JOHN

I was afraid you weren't in. I was just going to go away.

ROSS

I happen to be very busy, at the moment—

JOHN

Well, I'm awfully sorry to disturb you, Mr. Ross. But if
you'll just give me two minutes.

Ross

If you think you can put yourself through college by sell
ing me a subscription to the *Ladies' Home Journal,* you're
mistaken.

John

I've already been through college and, offhand, I wouldn'
pick you as a good prospect for the *Ladies' Home Journai*

Ross

I'm not a good prospect for anything, so if you're soliciting
my trade or my vote or my opinion on the European situation, you can save us both a lot of time by making a quiet
and swift departure.

John

I'd like to explain to you—

Ross

How did you get in here, anyhow? There's a strict rule
in this building against canvassing.

John

I'm not canvassing, Mr. Ross. I'm making personal visits
to a limited and selected list of professional men and
women, as a representative of the Fine Arts Publishing
Company—

Ross

That's a nice distinction. But the fact that you got my
name from some high-grade sucker list doesn't make you
any more welcome. So if you'll excuse me—

John

All I want is a chance to tell you about one of the most
attractive offers in the history of art publishing, an entirely new and original method—

Ross

(*Interrupting as* JOHN *starts to open his brief case*)
Don't open that, because I don't want to see it!

JOHN

But, Mr. Ross, all I ask is—

Ross

All I ask is that you get out of here on your own motive
power, before I throw you out.

JOHN

Well, I don't want to put you to all that trouble. So, I'll
just trot back to the office and ring up another "No Sale"
on the cash register. I'm sorry I came in at the wrong
moment. It's just that I'm trying to make a living, that's
all.

Ross

That's something in which you can hardly expect me to
take an interest.

JOHN

No reason why you should. I guess I'd feel the same way
if I were in your position. Only, I wish I knew where to
find a little spot of pasture land on this rocky island.
Ringing the doorbells of the great is getting me nowhere.

Ross

Look, if you want to talk about your career, that's one
thing, but—

JOHN

No, no, I'm on my way! Excuse me for taking so much
of your time and thanks for giving me an idea of how
to live when I bring in that gusher of mine.

(*He exits and closes the door behind him.* Ross *stands
looking at the door, for a moment, then shrugs his*

*shoulders and crosses to the bedroom. The door opens
and* MARY *enters, dressed for the street.*)

ROSS

I see. Clothed and in your right mind. I thought I told
you I had to finish that drawing today.

MARY

I'm terribly sorry, Mr. Ross, but I'll have to ask you to
excuse me.

ROSS

Well, I guess there's not much I can do about it, is there,
since you seem to be on your way out. How about tomorrow at eleven? I may be able to put them off for a
day.

MARY

I'm afraid I can't. I have an appointment with a manager
tomorrow morning.

ROSS

Shall we make it two-thirty, then?

MARY

Well—all right. Tomorrow at two-thirty.

ROSS

And in the morning, I'll get a telegram, informing me
that you've gone to Australia or that your aunt has come
down with trichinosis.

MARY

I'm afraid I couldn't afford a telegram.

ROSS

(*Laughing*)

Right on your toes, aren't you?

MARY

Mr. Ross, I hate to ask it of you, but if you could possibly pay me for this week's work. We won't count today, since I'm not staying to finish—

Ross

Certainly, we'll count today.

(*He takes out his wallet.*)

Let's see. Three hours Monday. Three hours yesterday—

Mary

And two hours today, since you're kind enough—

Ross

That makes eight hours. Let's call it thirty dollars.

(*He hands her three ten-dollar bills.*)

Mary

No, of course not. Eight times three are twenty-four. I owe you six dollars.

(*She takes the change out of her purse.*)

Ross

Oh, forget it!

Mary

(*Putting the money on the couch*)

I'll leave it here.

(*Extending her hand*)

And good-by.

Ross

(*Taking her hand in both his*)

Mary—

Mary

Please, Mr. Ross—!

Ross

I just want to say that I like you a lot. And that I think you really are a nice girl.

MARY

Well, I like you, too. So I think it's better for us to say
good-by, while we still like each other. What are you
laughing at?

Ross

Well, you are probably the only girl in the history of the
human race whose honor was saved by a strolling book
agent.

MARY

What do you mean by that?

Ross

Never mind!

(*He kisses her, lightly.*)

Good luck! And let me know next time you're opening
in a play.

MARY

I'll do more than that. I'll send you tickets. Good-by.

(*She goes out.*)

Curtain

Scene 6

The Coffee Pot, a modest eating place. At the right, is the entrance door from the street and just above it, a small cashier's desk. Parallel with the back wall is a counter, the right end curving back to the wall near the cashier's desk. The counter does not run all the way across, there being sufficient space at the left end to permit the counterman to go back and forth. In front of the counter are six or eight high stools on pivots. On the counter are several cake stands with glass covers, containing pies, cakes, and so on; also various condiments. Behind it is a shelf which contains crockery and cutlery and a coffee boiler. In the foreground, across the stage, are four booths, back to back, separated by low partitions. Each booth consists of two short benches with a table between them. On each table are salt and pepper shakers, a sugar bowl and a rack of paper napkins.

At the rise of the curtain BRODSKY, *the taxi driver, is seated in the booth at the extreme right, reading a book, and drinking coffee. At the right end of counter are* THE DRIVER *and* THE GUIDE *of the sightseeing bus. The latter is struggling with a crossword puzzle, between mouthfuls of food. The second booth from the right is occupied by* THE LITTLE MAN *with the portable radio and* HIS WIFE. *They are finishing their pie and coffee, and each is absorbed in the comic strips of a tabloid. On the table between them is the radio, from which music is heard.* JOHN,

*who is the counterman of the restaurant, dressed in a white
apron and starched white turban, is collecting some used
dishes and wiping up the table where* BRODSKY *is seated.
In the third booth, facing the door, is* SONIA TARANOVA, *a
dark, intense, hatless girl. She is reading the* New Masses
*and has before her a half-eaten sandwich and a cup of
coffee. Every few moments, she glances anxiously toward
the door. In the fourth booth is* GRACIE MULLEN, *a cheaply
pretty redhaired girl. Seated beside her is the sailor,*
DIXIE BUSHBY. *He is showing her some snapshots.*

DIXIE

(*Handing* GRACIE *a snapshot*)
How do you like that for a shape?

GRACIE

Say, it's no wonder you guys enlist in the Navy.

DIXIE

(*Laughing*)
I'll say. But personally, I prefer 'em redheaded.
  (*He puts his hand on her knee.*)

GRACIE

Yeah?
  (*She slaps his hand.*)
Make your hands behave, sailor!

DIXIE

(*Rubbing his hand*)
Hey, what's the big idea?

GRACIE

Under the table is out, if you get what I mean.
  (*Taking the snapshots from him*)
Here, I can look at those alone. You finish your rice
pudding.

THE LITTLE MAN

Wanna go?

HIS WIFE

May as well.

(*He picks up the radio, and they go to the cashier's desk, pay their checks and exit.*)

THE GUIDE

(*To* THE DRIVER)

Say, what's an elonjated fish in three letters?

THE DRIVER

How the hell should I know? Ask the Perfesser.

THE GUIDE

(*Calling to* BRODSKY)

Hey, Four-Eyes, what's an elonjated fish in three letters?

BRODSKY

(*Looking up*)

An elonjated fish in three letters? That's simple. Eel.

THE GUIDE

Eel? Is an eel a fish? I thought it was a snake.

BRODSKY

That's a very common error. An eel is a fish, only without scales.

THE GUIDE

Wait a minute.

DIXIE

(*To* JOHN, *behind the counter*)

Hey, buddy, gimme a hunk o' that lemon meringue pie.

JOHN

O. K.

THE GUIDE

E-e-l. That makes a color r-e-d. Yeah, that fits all right.

(*He goes on with the puzzle.* BRODSKY *goes back to his book.*)

DIXIE

Hey, how much longer are we gonna wait for that dame?

GRACIE

She'll be here right away. I guess she got held up at the store.

(ORMONT *enters with* HELEN, *his wife, a sensitive-looking woman, with a rather faded prettiness. They go to the second booth.*)

ORMONT

Shall we sit here?

HELEN

Yes. Anywhere.

(*They sit opposite each other.* JOHN *serves the pie to* DIXIE *and goes over to the* ORMONTS.)

ORMONT

(*Not recognizing* JOHN)

I just want some coffee. What will you have, darling?

HELEN

Nothing for me.

ORMONT

You'd better have a little something.

HELEN

I really don't—All right, coffee.

JOHN

Two coffees.

(*He removes the soiled dishes and goes back to the counter. During the following, several* MEN *drift in and take places at the counter.*)

BRODSKY

(*Looking up from his book*)

Snakes are members of the reptile family and much higher animals than fishes.

THE GUIDE

Whaddye mean animals? Are you trying to tell me that fishes are animals?

BRODSKY

I am referring to the animal kingdom. That includes everything that has a nervous system. Butterflies, worms, alligators, oysters, everything.

THE GUIDE

Oysters are animals, too?

BRODSKY

By all means, oysters are animals.

THE GUIDE

Well, you may be right, but, personally, I never met a nervous oyster. How about it, Charlie?

THE DRIVER

Aw, that guy's a screwball.

THE GUIDE

Say, what do you do, sit up all night, reading the dictionary?

BRODSKY

I get the impression that you are not acquainted with the theory of evolution.

THE GUIDE

You mean like they got in Russia? What's that got to do with oysters?

BRODSKY

(*Disgustedly*)

Excuse me, but I got to concentrate.

(*He goes back to his book.*)

THE GUIDE

Oh, pardon my glove, Einstein. You better be careful, or they'll have you cutting out paper dolls, soon.

ORMONT

We seem to have strayed into the seminar of Biology One.

HELEN

Why do we come here, of all places?

ORMONT

I like it. Would you hear such a conversation at Twenty-One? Besides, when you're taking nothing, it's cheaper here than at the Ritz.

(JOHN *has come from behind the counter and serves them.*)

JOHN

You don't seem to remember me, Mr. Ormont.

ORMONT

You're quite right. Should I?

JOHN

No, I suppose not. I brought you a play to read about a year ago, when I first came to New York.

ORMONT

Well, that hardly identifies you.

JOHN

We had quite a little talk at the time. You promised to read the play. But I guess you never got around to it. It was a play about the dust bowl, called *Red Cloud*.

ORMONT

Oh yes, it comes back to me. So it's you, is it—the Euripides of the Corn Belt! As a matter of fact, I did read the play in a moment of absent-mindedness. As I recall it, it had magnificent potentialities of failure.

JOHN

Yes, that's what everybody seemed to think. No box office. But I've learned a lot about the theater since I've been in New York, and I've finished a new one, a comedy that I think has much more popular appeal than *Red Cloud*. You'd probably find a copy on your desk, if you cared to look.

ORMONT

Thanks. But I'm beginning to lose my youthful curiosity. And meanwhile, you amuse yourself by acting as maître d'hôtel of this chic little *boîte*.

JOHN

This is the only job I've been able to find that's even half-way permanent. I've sold two or three little stories but that's not enough to keep me going. Well, I'm sorry I talked so much.

HELEN

Oh, please don't apologize!

(JOHN *goes back to the counter.*)

ORMONT

The American cycle! The grandfathers drove their covered wagons across the Western plains, burning with the vision of an earthly Paradise—and now the corn-fed grandsons, dreaming of a new Athens, are hitch-hiking back to juggle saucers in a hash-house. O Pioneers!

HELEN

You might, at least, have given him a little encouragement.

ORMONT

Why? Why is it my function to give encouragement to callow young poets from the Mississippi Valley?

HELEN

Just for that reason. Because he's young and sensitive and ambitious. And because a little kindness and sympathy would mean so much to him. It means so much to everybody. Is it so hard to give?

ORMONT

Did I ask him to write plays? Did I bid him put down the plow and take the topless towers of New York by storm? If he doesn't like it here, why the hell doesn't he go back where he came from? It's charming of you to feel a tenderness for this rustic young Apollo, but myself, I am somewhat deficient in the maternal instinct.

HELEN

Yes, I know. That's really what's at the bottom of it all, isn't it? Because you've been hurt and feel defeated, you no longer have any pity for others. You enjoy watching them suffer—yes, enjoy making them suffer.

ORMONT

Freud is dead, darling. Aged eighty-three. Peace to his ashes!

HELEN

You didn't used to be like this, Larry. New York has done this to you. You had to succeed, no matter how, no matter whom you hurt. And when success came it was too much for you. You lost your head and your heart, too. Now you're going through a period of failure and you have nothing left inside you. You've thrown away all that was fine and creative in you. There's nothing there now but cruelty and cynicism.

ORMONT

What are you trying to do—destroy me altogether? Rob me of the last shred of self-respect? Damn all women! You're all alike. Possession, possession—that's all that matters to you. You'd rather see a man dead than give up your exclusive ownership in him.

HELEN

That's not true. I can put up with unfaithfulness; I've taught myself to do that. But not with complete neglect, complete indifference. How much longer do you expect me to go on like this—sitting up there, in the country, day after day, waiting for you to telephone that you won't be home? You haven't been home all week, and if I hadn't come down, I might not have seen you for another week.

ORMONT

Well, why don't you move into town? I'm no commuter.

HELEN

It wouldn't be any different in town. You know that. And I wouldn't even have my garden and the long walks over the back roads.

ORMONT

You don't want to live in the country; you don't want to live in New York. Do you want a yacht?

HELEN

All I want is to feel that I have a husband—not just somebody who's legally married to me, but a husband.

ORMONT

I'm in the theatrical business. I have to go and meet people, get around and see what's going on. Do you want me
to punch a time clock?

HELEN

No, I don't. Please give me credit for a little intelligence,
Larry. If I don't mean anything to you, any more, then
tell me so, honestly, so that I can know how to live my
life.

ORMONT

(*Clasping his brow*)

God! What have I done that everybody has to crucify
me?

(*He closes his eyes and averts his head.* HELEN *looks at
him in silence.*)

DIXIE

(*To* JOHN)

Hey, buddy, let's have another hunk o' pie.

GRACIE

Say, there's certainly nothin' the matter with your appetite.

DIXIE

Well, what the hell, there ain't nothin' else to do till that
dame gets here.

BRODSKY

(*Looking up from his book*)

I was reading only the other day about the Age of Reptiles,
when they were the biggest things on earth.

THE GUIDE

You don't tell me! When was that, Perfessor?

BRODSKY

Well, I wouldn't want to say exactly. Two or three million years ago.

THE GUIDE

No wonder I don't remember it. You mean all the big shots was snakes?

BRODSKY

Not snakes. Dinosaurs—Diaplodicus and Brontisaurius.

THE GUIDE

No foolin'!

BRODSKY

They were bigger than elephants, but their brains were microcospic. That's why they died.

THE GUIDE

Whaddye know! Hear that, Charlie?

THE DRIVER

Aw, he's nuts!

BRODSKY

That was millions of years before there were any men.

THE GUIDE

Gee, that must of been tough on the dames. Come on, Charlie, the hicks from Kansas are waiting for us to show 'em the perils of Gramercy Park.

(*Coming over to* BRODSKY)

You better lay off that wood alcohol, Four-Eyes, or one of them snakes is liable to bite your schnozzle off.

(BRODSKY *does not deign to reply.* THE GUIDE *and* THE DRIVER *pay their checks and exit.*)

DIXIE

Come on, whaddye say we go? I'm sick of hangin' around this dump.

GRACIE

Why don't you have another piece of pie?

DIXIE

I don't want no more pie. Say, Sandy's gonna bawl the hell out of me for keepin' him waitin' like this.

GRACIE

Just a couple o' minutes more, and if Mary ain't here by then, we'll go.

DIXIE

Aw, all right.

(WINTHROP *enters hurriedly, looks about, sees* SONIA, *and hastens toward her.*)

WINTHROP

I'm terribly sorry to be so late, Sonia.

SONIA

I've been sitting here for over an hour.

WINTHROP

Yes, I know, dear. But I've been busy until just now organizing the workers in the five-and-ten-cent stores.

(*To* JOHN)

Let me have a cup of coffee and a piece of sponge cake.

(*To* SONIA)

I've only got a few minutes. I have to go over to Brooklyn to address a meeting of the Dock Workers' Union, and I haven't even finished my notes for the speech.

(*Reaching across the table for her hand*)

I just couldn't help it, Sonia.

SONIA

(*Withdrawing her hand*)

It's the same thing every day. You don't give a damn how long you keep me waiting.

WINTHROP

You know as well as I do that I have to give the Party work precedence over everything else.

HELEN

Larry, dear—

ORMONT

No, you're right. I'm a flop, a has-been. Everything I touch turns rancid. I'm an also-ran, a flash in the pan. I thought I had something on the ball, but I was wrong. I got by on bluff. A new face and they fell for it. But now I'm a discontinued model, rusting on the junk heap. Nobody's to blame. I haven't got what it takes, that's all. I'm the victim of nothing but my own inner weakness. No character, no guts, no creativeness. A shallow monkey-mind and the amorality of a cretin. Final score: I've wrecked my life and I've wrecked yours.

HELEN

I can't listen to you when you talk like that. It's not you. It's New York. Larry, dear, let's go back. Let's go back to St. Louis.

ORMONT

What? Go back to St. Louis? Back to that crossroads hamlet at the junction of two muddy rivers? Are you crazy?

HELEN

No, I mean it. We were happy there. We could be happy again. Ruthie, too. She doesn't understand why you never come home. She loves you, Larry.

ORMONT

Ruthie! Yes, I should never have had a child. I blight whatever is near me.

HELEN

Everything would be different in St. Louis. They'd welcome you. You could open your Community Theater again —do fine things as you used to. You'd make a new reputation for yourself. You'd be free of all this cut-throat struggling that's wearing you out. It's too much for you, too much for anybody.

(*While she is speaking,* MARY *enters.*)

GRACIE

Here she is now.

(ORMONT *sees* MARY *and his attention wanders away from* HELEN. MARY *gives no sign of recognizing him. She looks about, sees* GRACIE *and goes toward her.*)

ORMONT

(*As* MARY *passes him*)

Hello, Mary.

MARY

(*Without stopping*)

Good evening, Mr. Ormont.

(HELEN *lapses into silence.*)

GRACIE

(*As* MARY *approaches*)

Well, for Gawd's sake, what happened to you? I thought you was never gonna get here.

MARY

There was some mix-up about the cash. I didn't think I'd ever get out of there.

GRACIE

Meet Dixie. I don't know his other name.

DIXIE

Bushby. I'm pleased to meet you.

MARY

How do you do, Mr. Bushby? Oh, it's good to sit down!

(BRODSKY *gets up, pays his check and exits.*)

JOHN

(*Coming over to* MARY)

Can I take your order?

MARY

I'd like some corn flakes with half-and-half. And a cup of coffee, please.

(JOHN *goes back to the counter.*)

GRACIE

Say, Mary, don't look now, but guess who's sitting in back of you?

MARY

Who?

GRACIE

That guy that was in the store today, talkin' to us about joinin' the union.

MARY

(*Not much interested*)

Oh, really.

GRACIE

Yeah, he was just tellin' his girl friend about it, only he didn't say nothing about how they threw him out on his ear.

(JOHN *comes back with* MARY'S *order.*)

HELEN

Who is that girl?

ORMONT

What girl?

HELEN

What girl! What girl do you suppose? The one who just came in.

ORMONT

Who is she? A girl. An actress. She played the maid in *Long Island Honeymoon*. Why?

HELEN

I thought I recognized her.

ORMONT

Remarkable powers of observation. And keen feminine intuition. Have I been intimate with her? No. Will I become intimate with her? Perhaps. We were talking about St. Louis, I believe, where they lock up the girls at curfew.

(HELEN *rises abruptly*.)

Are you leaving?

HELEN

I want to catch the nine-seventeen. Ruthie is expecting me.

ORMONT

I'll take you to the station.

HELEN

Don't bother.

ORMONT

It's no bother, darling.

(*They exit*.)

GRACIE

We're goin' dancin' at Roseland, Mary. We got a partner waitin' for you—friend o' Dixie's.

DIXIE

Yeah, Sandy Maxwell. Boy, can he step! He won two silver cups, last time we was in Panama.

Mary

I really can't, Gracie. My feet ache so that I couldn't even
drag myself around the floor, much less dance.

Dixie

(*Rising*)
Well, whaddye say we go?

Gracie

Wait a minute! Come ahead, Mary. A little steppin' and a
coupla drinks'll do you good.

Mary

No, I really couldn't. I'll see you at the store in the morning, Gracie. Good night, Mr. Bushby.

Dixie

Goo' night.
(*As he and* Gracie *go toward the door*)
Some tomater! Sandy'd bust me one in the beezer if I ever
brung her along.

Gracie

Aw, Mary's all right. She just ain't been in New York
long enough to get sophisticated, that's all.
(*As* Gracie *and* Dixie *exit,* Dorothy Clark *and* Clifton
Ross *enter, talking loudly. They are both in evening
dress and have had just enough to drink to make them
rather unrestrained.*)

Ross

We're going to miss most of the first act. Sure you don't
mind?

Dorothy

No, not a bit. I've seen the show three times. Anyhow,
Bea Lillie doesn't come on until the middle of the act.

Ross

(*Leading her to the first booth*)

Sorry to do this to you, Dot. But I just couldn't sit through any show on an empty stomach.

(*Everyone in the place is looking at them, as they seat themselves.*)

DOROTHY

Oh, but I think this is simply marvelous! I've always wanted to come to a place like this, but I've never been able to get anybody to take me.

(JOHN *comes over to take their order.*)

Ross

I recommend the chili. It's very good here.

DOROTHY

What is it?

Ross

Beans with pepper. It's a Mexican dish and they really know how to make it. Try it.

DOROTHY

All right, I will. It sounds wonderful.

JOHN

Two chilis?

Ross

Yes. And coffee with cream.

(*As* JOHN *starts to go*)

Wait a minute! Haven't I seen you somewhere, before?

JOHN

Yes, you have, Mr. Ross. I once tried to sell you some art publications but you weren't having any.

Ross

I thought so! I'm afraid I was a little short with you, that day. I hope you don't hold it against me.

JOHN

Why, you were comparatively gentle with me. I thought I'd better give up that business, before I got my nose broken by a slamming door.

Ross

You find it more congenial here?

JOHN

Yes, decidedly. The clients aren't as clever, but they have less sales resistance. I'll get your order, right away.

DOROTHY

Who is he?

Ross

A kid I threw out of my studio, one day. Remind me to tell you about it, later. It's really a very funny story, with a slightly Rabelaisian touch.

DOROTHY

I like his looks.

Ross

Yes, I noticed that.

DOROTHY

I'm simply mad about this place! What kind of people come here, Cliff?

Ross

Oh, I don't know. People who work in offices and shops, taxi drivers, policemen—just ordinary people.

DOROTHY

But it's fascinating. I'm so fed up with all those East Side joints. The same old dreary faces, day after day. Everybody you went to school with. Or a lot of dull little people you don't want to know. Even Harlem is getting to be awfully commercialized and synthetic. But this is really exciting. Promise me you'll take me to more places like this.

Ross

Nothing could be simpler. But we'll wear mufti, next time. I'm afraid we're just a little bit conspicuous.

Dorothy

Oh, I've got lots of old clothes that would just be ideal for this sort of thing.

(*As* John *approaches with the order*)

Oh, here's the whatever-you-call-it.

(*Smiling at* John.)

Thank you ever so much.

John

You're welcome. I hope you enjoy it.

Dorothy

Oh, I know I will. It looks marvelous.

(*As* John *serves them,* Heinz Kaltbart, *the Austrian refugee, enters with a stack of tabloids under his arm.*)

Kaltbart

Papers! Morning papers! *News! Mirror!* Morning papers!

(*He begins to make the rounds of the place.*)

News! Mirror! Morning papers!

Mary

News, please.

Kaltbart

Thank you very much.

Dorothy

Ooh, it's hot, isn't it?

Ross

Would you rather have something else? A hamburger,. maybe?

Dorothy

No, this is delicious!

Kaltbart

(*Coming back to the first booth*)

Morning paper? *News? Mirror?*

Ross

No.

(Kaltbart *exits.*)

God, but I'm hungry!

(*They eat, relapsing into silence.*)

Sonia

Damn them!

Winthrop

(*Startled out of his self-absorption*)

Who?

Sonia

Who! Who! Who do you think? Those bourgeois Park Avenue snobs, that's who!

Winthrop

Why get excited about them?

Sonia,

What right have they to come here slumming—looking us over, as if we were a lot of animals in the zoo. I'd like to go and tear the clothes off her back.

Winthrop

Why don't you exercise a little self-control? Put your energies into working for the movement instead of dissipating them in senseless emotion.

Sonia

You're telling that to me? To me? I'm working sixteen, eighteen hours a day for the movement, living on eight dollars a week. Some days I have only one meal. And you're telling me I should work for the movement!

Winthrop

All you're doing is indulging yourself in a childish emotional debauch. Why don't you acquire a little objectivity?

Sonia

Yes, objectivity! For you all this means only something that you've read about in books. But I come from the people. I've lived the life of the workers. My mother died of consumption in a stinking tenement, so that those class enemies could have lace dresses and ride in limousines. And you sit there like a fish and talk about objectivity!

Winthrop

I'm trying to make you see that personal hatred is an anarchistic deviation that has no place in the movement. It's not a handful of insignificant plutocrats that we're fighting, but a decaying system of which they are the products.

Sonia

That's right! Defend them! Stick up for them! Maybe you went to Harvard together and belong to the same golf club. Why don't you take her to the opera and go to bed with her afterward? Go ahead! I don't mind!

Winthrop

That's damned unfair! I never saw either of them before, and I think their manners are extremely bad. But if I may say so, yours are even worse.

SONIA

Of course! I know what you think of me. A girl from the
tenements, who should be honored if the rich Mr. Winthrop looks at her. Do you know what you are? Nothing
but a dirty snob, like all the rest of them.

WINTHROP

It's just a waste of time trying to talk to you, when you
get into one of these moods.

(*He goes back to his notes.*)

SONIA

(*Rising*)

I'm going. I'm tired of sitting here.

WINTHROP

(*Rising*)

Well, I'm sorry I can't go with you but I've got to get this
speech organized. Leave your check.

SONIA

I'll pay my own check. I'm not a charity case.

WINTHROP

All right, just as you like. Can you meet me tomorrow?

SONIA

I don't know.

WINTHROP

Let's say half-past six at the Co-op, and I'll try to be on
time. Good night.

SONIA

Good night.

(*She pays check at cashier's desk and exits, looking at*
Ross *and* DOROTHY. WINTHROP *looks after her, then
glances at* MARY *and resumes his seat.*)

DOROTHY

Honestly, this is the most heavenly food I've ever tasted. Do you know any other places like this?

ROSS

Oh, sure. New York is full of them. Have you ever been to any of the Jewish restaurants, down on lower Second Avenue?

DOROTHY

No, but I'd adore going. You know, you make me feel as if I really don't know a thing about New York.

ROSS

Say, we'd better go, or we won't see *any* of the first act. (*They rise and he helps her with her wrap.*)

DOROTHY

When are you going to give me another painting lesson? Tomorrow afternoon?

ROSS

Sure thing. When are you and I getting married?

DOROTHY

(*As they go toward the door*)

You know I don't want to get married again. Twice is plenty. For a while, anyhow.

ROSS

All right. I'll wait a while.

DOROTHY

Do you really think I have some talent for painting?

ROSS

Oh, definitely!

(*She waits as* ROSS *goes to pay the check.* JOHN, *meanwhile, approaches the booth.*)

DOROTHY

(*Smiling at him*)

Thank you. The chili was wonderful.

JOHN

Well, I'm glad you like it. Come in again.

DOROTHY

I certainly shall! Good night.

(*As she rejoins* ROSS)

I'm mad about that waiter.

ROSS

(*As they exit*)

I'll give him to you for Christmas.

(JOHN *goes to the vacated booth and begins to clear the table*. WINTHROP *rises and goes to* MARY.)

WINTHROP

Excuse me, I'm Frederic Winthrop. I was talking to you this afternoon about joining the Chain Store Workers' Union.

MARY

Oh, yes. How do you do?

WINTHROP

Do you mind if I sit down for a minute?

MARY

No, not if you want to.

WINTHROP

Thank you.

MARY

I'm sorry they were so rough with you. I hope you weren't hurt.

WINTHROP

No, just shaken up a little. I'm getting used to that sort of thing.

MARY

Well, you certainly have a lot of courage.

WINTHROP

It's nothing to what organizers in the metal industries have to face. Did I give you one of our union leaflets?

MARY

No, you didn't.

WINTHROP

Well, I have one right here.

(*Handing* MARY *a leaflet*)

Just look this over. It explains what the worker has to gain by joining the union.

MARY

I'm afraid I don't understand anything about this sort of thing.

WINTHROP

Well, let me clarify it for you.

MARY

But, you see, this job of mine in the five-and-ten is just temporary. I'm really not—

WINTHROP

Nevertheless, you are employed there. Now, first of all, let me describe briefly just what the Chain Store Workers' Union is. It's a regular trade union composed of white collar workers in all the chain stores throughout the country.

(*While he is speaking, a bulky, red-faced* MAN *enters.*)

The Man

(*Calling to John*)

Hey, feller, let's have a Western sandwich and a cup of Java.

John

Yes, sir.

(The Man *goes to the second booth and becomes absorbed in a pink racing form.*)

Curtain

Scene 7

A small exhibition room in the Metropolitan Museum of Art. At the right and left are wide entrance ways, leading to adjoining galleries. On the rear wall are hung examples of French painting of the late 19th Century: Cezanne, Van Gogh, Gauguin, Manet, etc. In the middle of the room, is a double bench, facing the back wall and the imaginary fourth wall.

At the rise of the curtain, MRS. BALLINGER, *a stout, elderly woman, is standing upstage right, lecturing to a group of five* WOMEN, *who sit huddled about on camp chairs, their backs to the audience. One of them is* MRS. LEVY. *Several of the women have notebooks.*

MRS. BALLINGER

(Talking as the curtain rises)

But today, of course, his paintings are prized by collectors and bring the most fabulous prices, though I must say I'd think twice about paying thirty or forty thousand dollars for one of them, even if I had it to spend. Well, I think that about disposes of Cezanne. The important thing for us to remember is that all of these painters—Cezanne, Van Gogh, Gauguin and all the other Impressionists—were trying to find new ways of saying things. That is, they weren't interested in telling a story in their paintings, but, as someone has said of Cezanne, for example, they were trying to show solid objects existing in space.

A Woman

Mrs. Ballinger, wasn't Van Gogh the one who cut off his own ears?

Mrs. Ballinger

Yes, he was. And Gauguin, you know, ran off to the South Seas and spent the rest of his life there. Just lighted out one day and never came back. But, of course, artists are very temperamental people. If they weren't, they couldn't be artists, I suppose. Now, as we go on, the paintings become queerer and queerer and harder and harder to understand. However, we must keep our judgment in abeyance, and not just say "Oh! Oh!" Now, these Impressionists were followed by a great many other schools—Cubism, Futurism, Pointillism, Expressionism, Vorticism, Surrealism, Dadaism—

A Woman

Not quite so fast, Mrs. Ballinger.

Mrs. Ballinger

Oh, don't bother about getting it all down now. Just remember to keep the whole thing very fluid in your minds. Now, let's go on to the next room, and there you'll see a Picasso that will startle you a little, I think.

(*As they all rise and pick up their camp chairs, she moves toward the doorway at the right, the others following.*)

I do wish we had more time to spend here, but we really must finish this French school today, because next week I want to get started on Chinese ceramics.

A Woman

Isn't it pronounced keramics?

MRS. BALLINGER

Well, some say keramics. But I prefer ceramics. After all, it's spelt with a "c." C-e-r, cer!

(*She exits followed by the other* WOMEN, *as* MARY *and* WINTHROP *enter at the left.* MRS. LEVY *brings up the rear of* MRS. BALLINGER's *students and* MARY *sees and recognizes her, just as she reaches the doorway.*)

MARY

(*Hurrying across the room*)

Hello, Mrs. Levy!

(MRS. LEVY *turns in surprise, then beams as she recognizes* MARY.)

MRS. LEVY

(*Taking* MARY's *hand*)

Hello! Hello! How are you? I'm so glad to see you again!

MARY

Well, I'm glad to see you. How have you been?

MRS. LEVY

Oh, I'm feeling so-so. I'm living now at the Hotel Cleveland, on West 83rd Street.

MARY

Oh, aren't you living with your daughter any more?

MRS. LEVY

No, it's better not for old people and young people to live together. They have their little apartment and their friends, so it's much better for me to have a room in an apartment hotel.

MARY

But isn't it awfully lonesome for you?

MRS. LEVY

Oh well, sometimes I feel a little bit lonesome. But I'm

very comfortable. I have a little kitchenette and I fix my own meals and it's very nice. Maybe you'll come and pay me a visit, some time.

MARY

Why yes, I'd love to.

MRS. LEVY

That would be fine! Well, I must go back to the class now. My daughter gave me Mrs. Ballinger's lecture course for a birthday present, so every Wednesday, I come here to the Museum.

MARY

And do you find it interesting?

MRS. LEVY

Well, she's a very fine woman, Mrs. Ballinger—with a wonderful education. Of course, some of it is a little beyond me. Well, I must go now.

(*Patting* MARY's *cheek*)

Good-by! I'm so glad to see you again.

MARY

Good-by, Mrs. Levy.

(MRS. LEVY *exits.*)

MARY

(*Rejoining* WINTHROP)

Poor old thing—living all by herself like that. Isn't it sad?

WINTHROP

Yes, it is.

(*They look at pictures.* JOHN *enters at the right as a uniformed* ATTENDANT *enters at the left.*)

JOHN

Say, did you happen to notice a lame man, with one of those high shoes, around here anywhere?

THE ATTENDANT

No, I didn't.

(*He exits right as* JOHN *exits left.*)

MARY

Oh, what a lovely little Degas! Come and look at this, Fred.

(WINTHROP *comes over beside her.*)

Isn't it charming?

WINTHROP

Historically very interesting.

MARY

What do you mean historically?

WINTHROP

It's an excellent example of a bourgeois culture that has fulfilled its historic role and is now in its decline.

MARY

But why can't you look at it as something that's just beautiful and exciting—something wonderfully rich and alive? Why does everything have to be mixed up with history and politics and all that?

WINTHROP

Art doesn't exist in a vacuum, Mary. Like everything else, it's conditioned by the society in which it flourishes. Degas employed an idiom that was peculiar to his time. But a dominant working class will find its own idiom.

MARY

Oh well, it's all too much for me.

(A MAN *and a* WOMAN *enter at the right and cross rapidly to the left.*)

THE WOMAN

All right, if you want to look at the paintings, you stay

here and look at them. I came to see the furniture in the
American Wing and that's what I'm going to see.

THE MAN

(*As they exit*)

Does that mean that you can't look at anything else?

MARY

Fred, I want to talk to you. Let's sit down for a minute.
(*They sit on the bench.*)
I've decided to take that part.

WINTHROP

But Mary, you said yesterday that it's a very bad play
that has no chance of success.

MARY

I know. But it just seems as though I'm not really interested in anything but acting, and I'd rather act in a ter-
rible play that's sure to flop than go on working in the five-
and-ten.

WINTHROP

Well, if you'll forgive my saying so, I don't think that's
very intelligent.

MARY

I guess *I'm* not very intelligent. That's what you really
mean, isn't it?

WINTHROP

No, of course, I don't. Only—

MARY

Well, I wouldn't blame you, if you did. Listen, Fred—I've
been thinking a lot about you and me and I think we'd
better call the whole thing off.

WINTHROP

But, Mary—!

MARY

No, I mean it! It just wouldn't work out for us. I know it wouldn't.

WINTHROP

I don't see why.

MARY

Because we're not interested in the same things. You think I'm wasting my time trying to be an actress. And I just can't seem to get excited about whether the girls at the store join the union or not. So we'd always be miles and miles apart.

WINTHROP

But as rational human beings, Mary, we can surely find—
(*While he is speaking, there is a commotion off stage right—a confusion of voices and the sound of rapid footsteps.*)

MARY

Wait! What's happening?
(*She rises as the* ATTENDANT *hurries on at the right.*)
Is anything wrong?

THE ATTENDANT

(*As he crosses*)
An old lady in the study class went into a faint. I'm going after a doctor.

MARY

Oh, I hope it's not Mrs. Levy! I must go and find out! Wait here, Fred.

WINTHROP

Mary—!

MARY

I won't be a minute!

(*She exits hastily at the right.* WINTHROP *goes back to the bench and slumps down, despondently.* ORMONT *enters at the left, with his daughter,* RUTH, *a sensitive, delicate child of twelve. They start to cross the room.*)

RUTH

Can't we look at these, Daddy?

ORMONT

Well, we haven't much time, Ruthie. Mother expects you at the station at four and you don't want to keep her waiting. And I'd like you to see the Picassos in one of the other rooms. Wait a minute! There's a little Degas that I want you to look at.

(*They come downstage and look at the painting.*)
Well, do you like it?

RUTH

Yes, it's nice.

ORMONT

A great painter, Degas. A man who understood life. Do you see how he uses color to build his forms? That's the difference between an artist and an illustrator. An illustrator just makes a drawing and then fills in the color. But to an artist, color and form are one. He uses his pigments plastically, almost in the way that a sculptor uses clay. Do you understand the difference?

RUTH

Yes. Daddy, do you think *I'll* ever be a great artist?

ORMONT

Why not? But it means hard work. Just having a gift for it isn't enough. Art is a discipline. You have to keep trying and trying—slashing up ten canvases and beginning over again, before you finish one picture. An artist's success is built upon his failures. If you want to be an artist, you must work and study.

RUTH

Yes, I know. Daddy, why aren't you coming to St. Louis with us?

ORMONT

Well, you know why, Ruthie. My work is here. When you're in the theatrical business, you have to stay in New York.

RUTH

Then why can't we stay in the East, too? I'd much rather be here where I can see you.

ORMONT

Well, mother thinks it will be better for you both to be out there. She likes St. Louis, and grandma and grandpa are getting old now, and she wants to be near them. And you'll like it, too.

RUTH

I won't, Daddy. I know I won't.

ORMONT

Yes, you will. You'll be going to school and to classes at the Art Institute. And you'll soon make a lot of new friends —more than you have here.

RUTH

But I'll never see you.

ORMONT

Well, we'll try to arrange that. We'll write to each other, often, and I'll call you up, every week or so.

RUTH

But that's not like *seeing* you. Will you come to see me, sometimes? Promise me you will.

ORMONT

Yes, if I can get away. And I'll tell you what I'll do. I'll have you come to New York to see me, every once in a while—Christmas and Easter holidays, maybe. That'll be nice, won't it?

RUTH

Yes.

ORMONT

We'll do the town together—go to the theaters and the art shows and raise hell generally. Does that appeal to you?

RUTH

Of course it does. Only you'll be busy and you won't have time.

ORMONT

Certainly, I'll have time! I'll always have time for you. Just you leave it to me and don't worry about it.

RUTH

(*Hesitantly*)
Daddy—

ORMONT

What?

RUTH

Are you and mother going to get a divorce?

ORMONT

Why, where do you get that idea?

RUTH

I don't know. Except that it always seems to be that way when married people go away from each other. That's the way it was with Ellen's parents and with Marie Crosby's, too. Please don't get a divorce, daddy.

ORMONT

Why, of course not! Married people often separate for a while without getting divorced. I don't want you to start brooding, Ruthie. Because if you do, you won't get on with your work. I want you to give all your attention to your studies and your painting and not start worrying about a lot of other things. Will you do what I ask you to?

RUTH

Yes, daddy.

ORMONT

(*Kissing her*)

That's right! Now let's take a quick look at the Picassos and then you have to get down to the station.

(*As they go right*)

Well, we've had a pretty nice day together, haven't we?

RUTH

(*As they exit*)

Oh, it's been lovely!

(*As* ORMONT *and* RUTH *exit at the right, the* ATTENDANT *hurries on at the left, followed by a* DOCTOR, *carrying an instrument case. They cross the stage quickly and exit at the right.* WINTHROP *turns and watches them.* ROSS *enters at the left.*)

JOHN

(*Following him on*)

Mr. Ross!

ROSS

(*Stopping and turning*)

Oh, it's you!

JOHN

I've been hunting all over the place for you. I have a message for you from Miss Clark.

Ross

What do you mean, a message? Isn't she here?

JOHN

No, she asked to be excused. She's been shopping all day and she has a headache.

Ross

You mean she's done this to me again? Keeping me waiting over an hour and then not showing up.

JOHN

She said she's awfully sorry.

Ross

Sorry, my eye! Well, you can take Miss Clark a message from me. Tell her I'm goddam sick and tired of her antics and she can go to hell.

JOHN

Well, I'd love to do that, if I hadn't just told her practically the same thing on my own account.

Ross

Good for you!

JOHN

Yes, I've just fired myself. I played up to her little ego just so long and then my old Middle-Western spirit of independence got the better of my economic interests. I guess I haven't got the right temperament for domestic service.

Ross

We seem to have a lot in common. What do you say we find some bar and drink death and damnation to all women?

JOHN

I'd rather be a little more specific, if you don't mind.

Ross

All right, whatever you say. Come on!

(*As they exit at the left,* MARY *hurries on at the right, wiping her eyes. She carries a slip of paper.*)

MARY

Fred, it *was* Mrs. Levy!

WINTHROP

What's happened?

MARY

She's dead. It was a heart attack. She died just before the doctor got here.

WINTHROP

It's shocking.

MARY

Come and help me find a phone. I've promised to call up her daughter. Such a sweet old lady!

(*They exit at the left. Two stolid-looking* JAPANESE MEN, *wearing horn-rimmed spectacles enter at the right. They come downstage and walk across the room, presumably glancing at the pictures and then coming to a halt before the Degas. They look at it for a moment, then look at each other and begin to giggle.*)

Curtain

Scene 8

A street in the West Forties. It is night and the sidewalk is lighted by an arc light which is off stage left. Near the right is the entrance to the Silver Bar, a popular night resort. Throughout the scene music is heard faintly from the bar. To the left of the brightly lighted entrance way is the dark façade of an office building. At the rise of the curtain WINTHROP, *carrying his inevitable brief case, appears at the left.* GRACIE *comes on at the right and approaches him with a mechanical smile.*

GRACIE

Hello, dear.

(WINTHROP *pays no attention to her and exits at the right. A* YOUNG MAN *appears at the left and* GRACIE *saunters up to him.*)

Hello, dear.

(THE MAN *walks past her, then stops and looks back. She turns quickly and walks back to him. They stand together close to the wall of the office building and engage in a whispered conversation.* ANOTHER MAN *comes along at the left as* JOHN *appears at the right.*)

JOHN

(*As* THE MAN *approaches him*)

Excuse me.

(THE MAN *stops.*)

Can you help me get something to eat?

(*Without replying,* THE MAN *walks past him and enters*

123

the bar. THE LITTLE MAN *with the portable radio comes out of the bar and goes off stage right.* JOHN *quickly follows him off.* DOROTHY CLARK *appears at the left, accompanied by a* HINDU *in a turban.*)

DOROTHY

Will there be many people at the meeting?

THE HINDU

No, Miss Clark. Not more than eight or ten. I invite only those who have the mentality and the inner preparedness to receive the truth.

DOROTHY

I can't tell you how thrilling it all is! Only there's one thing that I never can remember—just what the difference is between Karma and Nirvana.

THE HINDU

They are really quite different states. Karma is a condition of inner peacefulness which we can attain only through—
(His voice trails off, as they exit at the right. The MAN *who is talking to* GRACIE *shakes his head and goes off left.* GRACIE *saunters along to the right, as* ORMONT *comes out of the bar.*)

GRACIE

(With her mechanical smile)
Hello, dear.

ORMONT

I'm not casting.
*(*GRACIE *walks off right,* ORMONT *goes left as* MARY *enters from that direction. They meet in the center of the stage.*)

ORMONT

Hello, Mary!

MARY

(*Without stopping*)

Good evening, Mr. Ormont.

ORMONT

(*Turning and seizing her arm*)

Wait a minute! What are you running away for? Am I a leper?

MARY

It's late and I have to get home.

ORMONT

It's early and I want to talk to you. What are you doing now?

MARY

Looking for a job as usual.

ORMONT

I saw that last stinkaroo that you were in. Why do you do it?

MARY

Because it was the only thing I could get.

ORMONT

That's the silliest remark I ever heard. I thought you wanted to be an actress.

MARY

It gave me a chance to be seen.

ORMONT

So would doing a headstand in Times Square. Furthermore, your performance was just about as lousy as the play.

MARY

I'm sorry you think so. I got some good notices.

ORMONT

Where? In the *Iron Age*?

MARY

No, in two important papers. And all the others mentioned me.

ORMONT

A tribute to youth and to the absence of visible warts. Who directed that show, anyhow? The girl in charge of the ladies' room?

MARY

Well, he wasn't a very good director, I know that. And I realize how important it is to work with fine directors. But if they won't have you, what are you going to do?

ORMONT

Why haven't you been in to see me?

MARY

Well—
 (*She breaks off.*)

ORMONT

Well what?

MARY

I didn't think you'd have anything for me.

ORMONT

Maybe I wouldn't. And maybe I would. You never can tell. I'm funny that way. An erratic genius. Ask anybody on Broadway. A son-of-a-bitch net, but, boy, when he's right, there's nobody better.
 (*Taking her arm*)
Come and have a drink with me.

MARY

Thanks, but I really must get home.

ORMONT

I've got something I want to talk to you about.

MARY

It's awfully nice of you, Mr. Ormont, but I've really got—

ORMONT

You've really got to get home! You've really got to get home! There are four thousand girls in this town who would give their right eyes to talk to me about a part—and you've got to get home!

MARY

(*Troubled*)

You mean you think you might have a part for me?

ORMONT

What did you suppose I wanted to talk to you about—the quantum theory?

MARY

I didn't know you were doing a play.

ORMONT

Nobody knows it yet. It's a plausible script and it'll be still better if I can keep the author away from rehearsals. And there's a part in it that's so nearly actor-proof that I think I could get even you to give a performance in it.

MARY

Are you really serious about it, Mr. Ormont, or are you just—?

ORMONT

Listen, I have tender feet and a roving nature. Do you want to talk about this part or don't you?

MARY

A chance at a good part would mean just about everything in the world to me right now.

ORMONT

Then let's have a drink and talk it over.

(*He leads her toward the bar.*)

MARY

Maybe you'd rather I came to your office in the morning.

ORMONT

(*Stopping abruptly*)

You don't want to have a drink with me?

MARY

(*In a panic*)

Yes, of course I do! Only—

ORMONT

Then, go ahead!

(*He leads her into the bar.* JOHN *enters at the right, eating salted peanuts from a small bag. He resumes his stand near the entrance to the bar. A* MAN *and a* WOMAN *enter at the left.* JOHN *approaches them.*)

JOHN

(*To* THE MAN)

Excuse me.

(*They stop.*)

THE MAN

Yes, sure.

JOHN

I'm trying to collect enough to feed myself for the next twenty-four hours. Could you possibly help me out?

(*The* MAN *reaches into his pocket.*)

THE WOMAN

Wait a minute! Don't give him anything!

(*To* JOHN)

Why don't you get a job—a big, husky man like you?

JOHN

If you know of any job that's open, I'd be only too glad to—

THE WOMAN

If you can't find a job, why don't you go on relief?

JOHN

I'd rather work for what I get.

THE WOMAN

Do you call this work? Begging on the streets!

JOHN

I certainly do! If you don't believe me, try it yourself some time.

THE WOMAN

Well, of all the impudence—! I should think a big fellow like you would be ashamed of himself to—

THE MAN

(*Dragging her away*)

Oh, come on, Mabel!

(*He sheepishly offers* JOHN *a coin.*)

Here.

JOHN

Thanks a lot, but I'd rather not.

THE MAN

O.K.

THE WOMAN

(*As they enter the bar*)

Why do you encourage people like that? A cheeky good-for-nothing who would rather beg than try to make an honest living.

THE MAN

He looked all right to me.

(GRACIE *strolls on at the right and comes up to* JOHN.)

GRACIE

Hello, dear.

JOHN

Hello.

GRACIE

Have you got the time?

JOHN

(*Laughing*)

I'm out here myself, trying to scare up the price of a couple of meals.

GRACIE

No kiddin'?

(*Looking him over*)

You don't look like a panhandler.

JOHN

I know. I guess I'd do better if I looked more down-and-out. But if I gave up this suit, I wouldn't even have a chance of getting a job.

GRACIE

Well, if I had it to spare, I'd give you a dime. But all I got is ninety cents and I need it.

(*She starts to walk off left.*)

JOHN

Thanks just the same.

GRACIE

(*Stopping and turning back*)

Say, didn't you used to work in Joe's Coffee Pot on Eighth Avenue?

JOHN

Yes. That's right.

GRACIE

I thought I reckernized you. I used to eat in there, once in a while. I been workin' for two years in the five-and-dime, but whenever business gets bad, I get laid off. I don't do this regular, only when I'm not workin'.

JOHN

Looks like we're in the same boat, doesn't it? I don't do this regularly either, but I've got a good, hearty appetite and when I get too hungry, I can't work.

GRACIE

I thought you didn't have no job.

JOHN

Oh, those jobs, like working at Joe's, are just to fill in. My real work is writing.

GRACIE

(*Impressed*)

Yeah?

JOHN

Yes. I sold two stories last month, but they only pay on publication and I can't wait that long to eat. I could hock my typewriter, I guess, but if I did, I couldn't turn out any more stories and then where would I be?

GRACIE

Well, what's on my mind is where am I goin' to sleep to-night.

JOHN

Haven't you got a room?

GRACIE

No. The lan'lady threw me out last week. If I don't hook some guy, I'll have to sleep in the subway, I guess. I did that last night and it makes you feel pretty crummy.

JOHN

Well, if you've got ninety cents—

GRACIE

I gotta eat, too, don't I? Fifty cents for a room, that leaves forty to last me till tomorrow night. And then what if I don't have no luck? I must've walked about ten miles tonight, and I ain't had nothin' but a cup o' coffee since this mornin'.

JOHN

Have some peanuts.

(*He pours some into her hand.*)

GRACIE

Thanks. Boy, what I could do to a hamburger with onions! Say, there's a cop comin'. Let's make believe like we're talkin'.

(*As a* POLICEMAN *appears at the right*)

Which way do I go to get the Nint' Avenue El?

(THE POLICEMAN *strolls past, glancing at the pair.*)

JOHN

(*Very deliberately*)

The Ninth Avenue El? Well, you go along this way two blocks and then you turn to your left and walk three blocks down to the station.

(THE POLICEMAN *has now disappeared at the left.*)

GRACIE

Thanks. Well, I guess I better be on my way.

(*She starts to go left.*)

JOHN

Wait a minute.

GRACIE

(*Nervously*)

If that cop comes back, he'll run me in, and that means ten days in the workhouse. They got me once that way.

JOHN

Well, I've got a room that's paid for until the end of this week, and I was going to suggest that you're welcome to stay there tonight, if you like.

(*As* GRACIE *starts to protest*)

Don't misunderstand me. This is strictly business. You have ninety cents. I have forty-three. That makes a dollar thirty-three. The two of us could keep going on that until the day after tomorrow. Maybe by then one of us will find a job. Meanwhile, we'd both have enough to eat and you'd have a place to sleep.

GRACIE

And how about you? Where do you sleep?

JOHN

Well, I work all night and sleep in the daytime. I live in a house filled with howling kids and strong-lunged women, and I can't do a lick of work during the day.

GRACIE

And I'm supposed to sleep with you sittin' next to me, bangin' away at a typewriter all night?

JOHN

No, no! I do my stories in longhand. The typewriter is only for copying them. You won't even know I'm there.

GRACIE

Well, I don't know. I never had a proposition like that before.

JOHN

All right, just as you like. It would take us both off the
sidewalk for forty-eight hours, anyhow, and I thought
that might appeal to you.

GRACIE

You're goddam right it does.

(*Meanwhile A* MAN *has come out of the bar and is going
to the left.*)

Wait a minute!

(*She follows* THE MAN *off left.* JOHN *stands, watching
her, as* ORMONT *and* MARY *come out of the bar.*)

ORMONT

Which way do you go?

MARY

I—

ROSS

(*Appearing at the door of the bar*)

Larry! Just a minute!

ORMONT

(*To* MARY)

Wait a second.

(*He steps inside.* MARY *stands irresolute. She does not
notice* JOHN. *But his attention has been attracted to her.
He looks at her for a moment, then approaches her
hesitantly, as* GRACIE *appears at the left.*)

GRACIE

O.K. Let's go!

JOHN

(*Turning*)

Oh! Yes, all right.

(*He goes left and joins her.*)
We go this way.

GRACIE

Remember now—don't try to pull nothin'!

JOHN

(*As they go off left*)
If you change your mind when you get there, there's nothing to prevent your leaving, is there?

MARY

(*To* ORMONT, *who has come out of the bar*)
Oh, Mr. Ormont, I was just going to tell you not to bother. I haven't far to go.

ORMONT

So much the better.

MARY

I'd rather you didn't. I'm ashamed to have anyone see the place I'm living in.

ORMONT

When you write your memoirs for the *Saturday Evening Post,* you'll brag about it.
(*Linking his arm through hers*)
Where is it?

MARY

(*Weakly*)
West 54th Street.

ORMONT

We'll get a cab at the corner.

MARY

We could walk. It's not far.

ORMONT

If we ride, it won't be far, either.

(*They go off at the right. There is a commotion as* Two Waiters *eject a* Drunken Man *from the bar.*)

THE MAN

Lemme alone, I tell you! Lemme alone or I'll sock you one.

ONE OF THE WAITERS

Outside, please. Just go outside and stay outside, if you please.

(THE POLICEMAN *appears at the left and quickens his pace as he sees the altercation.*)

Curtain

ACT THREE

Scene 9

The top of the Statue of Liberty, viewed from the outside.
We see the eyes, the brow, the coiffure and the radiating
spikes of the crown. In the brow are the windows which
frame the hemispherical observation gallery. These win-
dows diminish in size as they curve away from the center.
The two middle ones are just wide enough to accommo-
date two persons each; the others give room only for one.
The gallery is only about ten feet wide and at most can
hold thirty-five or forty persons. At the back, on the right,
a spiral staircase, invisible to the audience, affords the
means of ascent. A similar staircase at the left is reserved
for descent.
As the curtain rises, a MIDDLE-AGED MAN *comes up the stairs,*
followed by TWO WOMEN.

THE MAN
(*As he reaches the gallery*)
O.K., girls! Here we are! This is the crown.

THE FIRST WOMAN
You mean to tell me this is the head, after all that walking?

THE SECOND WOMAN
Oh, my heart is going a mile a minute!

THE FIRST WOMAN
They say it's much easier coming up than going down.

THE SECOND WOMAN

Say, isn't it a gorgeous view, though?

THE MAN

I'll say. Must be the way it looks from an airplane.

A SLENDER WOMAN

(*Coming up the stairs*)

All right, Henry, this is the top. Come along!

A STOUT MAN

(*Puffing up the steps*)

I'm coming just as fast as I can.

(*He staggers into view.*)

Wee, that's a hike! I gotta take a rest.

THE SLENDER WOMAN

It wasn't so bad.

THE STOUT MAN

Don't forget you weigh a hundred and eight, and I weigh two twelve.

(JOHN *has come up the steps and taken a place at one of the windows.*)

THE SLENDER WOMAN

Oh, look at the arm, will you? I wonder if you can go up in it.

THE FIRST MAN

No. It's closed. I asked the elevator man.

THE STOUT MAN

Well, this is all the higher I want to go.

THE FIRST MAN

We'd better get going, girls, if we want to make that boat.

THE SECOND WOMAN

I'm scared that going down's going to be worse.

THE FIRST MAN

If you go down backward, you won't see where you're going.

(*They start to descend.*)

THE SLENDER WOMAN

Come on, Henry.

THE STOUT MAN

All right. I'm coming. I don't see why they couldn't make those stairs a little wider, though.

THE SLENDER WOMAN

Well, I think it's wonderful to be able to get up here at all.

(*As they descend, a* YOUNG HONEYMOON COUPLE *ascend,* THE GIRL *leading.*)

THE GIRL

Oh my! I didn't think I'd ever make it.

THE BOY

(*Anxiously*)

Are you all right, honey?

THE GIRL

Well, I feel kind of a little woozy.

(*She leans against his shoulder.*)

THE BOY

You'll be all right in a minute.

(*He kisses her.*)

Say, look at the view, will you!

THE GIRL

I don't like looking out. It makes me dizzy. Say, we ought to find a place to write our names.

THE BOY

Yes, all right.

(*They examine the girders and window frames.*)
Looks like there've been an awful lot of people up here.
Look, here's one goes way back to eighteen ninety-five.

THE GIRL

What do you know about that! Here's a place, right here.
Have you got a pencil?

THE BOY

Yeah. What'll I write?

THE GIRL

Well, I think it would look kind of cute to make two
hearts—you know, with one sort of over the other.

THE BOY

Oh, I know what you mean. Like that?
(MARY *comes up the stairs and takes a place at one of
the windows.*)

THE GIRL

Uh-huh! Now write Fred in one and Dolly in the other.
And the date underneath. Oh, that looks awfully cute.
And some day we'll come back and find it here, won't
we, darling?

THE BOY

(*Kissing her*)
You bet we will.

THE GIRL

Let's go down, Fred. I get a funny feeling being up here.

THE BOY

All right, honey.

THE GIRL

They say it's much worse going down.

THE BOY

You'll be all right. Look, I'll go first and you hold on to me.

THE GIRL

(*As they start to descend*)

I'm scared, darling.

THE BOY

Nothing to be scared of. I won't let you fall. Just keep hold of me.

(*As* MARY *watches them go off, she catches* JOHN's *eye. She averts her head and looks at the view.* JOHN *hesitates a moment, then strolls over beside her.*)

JOHN

Pretty impressive, isn't it?

MARY

(*Giving him a quick look*)

Yes, isn't it.

JOHN

Your first visit?

MARY

Yes, it is.

JOHN

I've been up here three or four times. So if there's anything I can point out to you—

MARY

Well, I was just sort of letting myself be overwhelmed by the whole picture. But it *would* be nice to know what some of the places are.

JOHN

Well, the big island there with the hills is Staten Island.

MARY

It somehow doesn't look like New York.

JOHN

No, it doesn't when you get there, either. They say there are people living there who have never been to Manhattan.

MARY

Well, look at me. I've been living in Manhattan for over two years and I never even knew where Staten Island is.

JOHN

Well, you haven't missed much. But on one of those hot summer nights, the ferry ride over from the Battery is the best nickel's worth in town.

MARY

Is that all it costs—a nickel?

JOHN

Yes. Municipal ferry. Look, there's one of the boats now. That big red tub. See it?

MARY

Oh yes! And what's that large white boat? That must be an ocean liner.

JOHN

I think she's on the South American service. I wouldn't mind being on her, right this very minute.

MARY

Oh, neither should I! I want to travel like mad and I'm going to some day, too—though goodness knows when or how.

JOHN

Well, as far as I've got is reading the travel folders. If you can't have the real experiences, it helps a little to imagine yourself having them.

MARY

Yes, I know.

JOHN

Tell me, where have I seen you before?

MARY

(*Looking at him*)
Is that a line? Because I was really enjoying the illustrated lecture.

JOHN

If that's what I were doing, I'd try to think up something a little more original. You don't remember ever seeing me?

MARY

Sorry. But I don't.

JOHN

Well, I've seen you. But I'll be damned if I can remember where. I'll think of it in a minute. All right, let's get back to Brooklyn.

MARY

Yes, that's a wonderful idea. Is that Brooklyn straight ahead?

JOHN

Yes, that's all Brooklyn.

MARY

I'm ashamed to say I've never been to Brooklyn either. Unless Coney Island is Brooklyn.

JOHN

Well, technically speaking it is. Seeing Brooklyn is a career in itself. As nearly as I can figure out, it's about as complicated as China. They even speak different languages in different parts of it. But I've been around a little: Williamsburg, Flatbush, Columbia Heights, the Navy Yard—

MARY

It sounds fascinating. I wish I had the energy to go around like that.

JOHN

Well, I wasn't going entirely on my own energy. For a while I was driving a delivery truck for a bakery on Atlantic Avenue.

MARY

Oh, were you?

JOHN

Well, truck driving isn't really my profession. Just sort of an avocation.

MARY

Well, that's what I thought.

JOHN

Thanks. Some of the time I go through the motions of pretending I'm a writer. I've got it!

MARY

What?

JOHN

Ormont!

MARY

Ormont?

JOHN

Yes, that's where I saw you—coming out of the Silver Bar with Larry Ormont. Late one night—two or three weeks ago. Somebody called him back and for a moment you stood there alone. Remember?

MARY

Yes, but I—do you know Larry Ormont?

JOHN

A little. I almost spoke to you.

MARY

Why to me?

JOHN

Just that you looked like the kind of a girl who might give a panhandler a dime.

MARY

A panhandler? You mean you were—?

JOHN

Yes. Begging. You look shocked.

MARY

No. I'm shock-proof by now. But a little surprised.

JOHN

Yes, I know. I guess I don't look that part, either. Maybe that's why I've never made a great success of it.

MARY

It sounds as if you've been having fierce hard luck.

JOHN

Well—that's charitable of you. Are you convinced now that I've seen you before?

MARY

Yes. Thoroughly convinced. But

JOHN

Good! Just so long as I've re-established myself as a lecturer without ulterior motives. That low, flat place is Governor's Island.

MARY

What do you write—stories?

JOHN

Yes. Cent-a-word for the pulps. But I had intentions of being a playwright.

MARY

So that's how you happen to know Ormont?

JOHN

Yes. That's Battery Park, where you took the boat.

MARY

He won't buy your plays?

JOHN

Nobody will buy my plays. Ever been to the Aquarium?

MARY

No. My name's Mary Ward.

JOHN

John Thompson.

MARY

My grandmother was a Thompson. Do you spell it with a "p"?

JOHN

Yes. My folks came from Massachusetts—about a hundred years ago.

MARY

Well, so did grandmother's family. Around North Adams, I think.

JOHN

Maybe we're related.

MARY

That's a thought.

JOHN

By the way, have you ever met anyone who was born in New York?

MARY

No, I don't think I have.

JOHN

Neither have I.

MARY

There must be some, though.

JOHN

Yes, there certainly must be. You know, of all the New York days I've known, I like these clear October ones best.

MARY

So do I. Only they get me thinking a little wistfully about the lovely New Hampshire woods—all the colors of the rainbow, now.

JOHN

Well, if I were back in Iowa today, I'd be out in corduroys and a wind-breaker, hunting rabbits over the corn stubble and the frozen lumps of brown earth.

MARY

Listen, I haven't very much money of my own but if you're broke, I can lend you a little—five dollars or so.

JOHN

Well, thanks! But I'm comparatively rich. This morning I collected seventy-five dollars for two stories I sold some time ago.

MARY

Seventy-five dollars!

JOHN

It happens I have only fifty left. I gave twenty-five to a girl who helped me out when I needed help. But that leaves more than enough to get me back to Iowa.

MARY

Oh, you're going to Iowa?

JOHN

Yes. Tomorrow morning. That's why I've come up here.
To kiss New York good-by.

MARY

You mean you're going for good?

JOHN

Well, for better or worse. You know, it's a funny thing—
but that skyline still gets me. I've seen so much of what
goes on behind that magnificent front that I thought I'd
developed an immunity to it.

MARY

Why are you going back home?

JOHN

I'm going into business with my brother. He has the
Chevrolet agency in Waterloo and he's been urging me to
come back ever since I landed in New York, over two
years ago.

MARY

Well, my folks keep urging me to come back, too, but I'll
never go back, no matter what I have to do to stay here.
New York's got me, I guess.

JOHN

That's what I'm afraid of—that it'll get *me*. Have you ever
been on the Bowery?

MARY

Yes. I took one of those sightseeing trips.

JOHN

I've been there often. A lot of promising boys there, who
put off going home until it was too late and they were

ashamed to go. I don't want to slouch along under the El, and be a guinea pig in a hair-cutting college.

MARY

But if you have fifty dollars—!

JOHN

Yes, I can live for four weeks on that—six if I have to. By that time, I might sell another story or get a job somewhere.

MARY

Yes, of course, you will!

JOHN

But I might not sell another story. Or I might not find a job—not even washing dishes. It'll be rainy next month, and then the cold weather begins. So far, I've always managed to hang on to my typewriter and one fairly decent suit of clothes. Next time, I don't know. And if I were hungry enough, I might not even hold out a few dollars for room rent. That would mean nights in flophouses or in the subway. And pretty soon, I'd begin to get a little careless about shaving, and not bothering much when buttons started falling off.

MARY

But, listen—

JOHN

Well, let's skip it. How did we ever get started on this, anyhow?

MARY

Well, we were just talking and—

JOHN

And the old male ego suddenly ran amok. You you're an awfully good listener. God knows, I struck any of those since I landed here.

MARY

Well, neither have I! Back home there'd always be somebody who cared enough to listen, but here—well, you know
how it is. Honestly, I sometimes don't know what to do
with myself—just longing for somebody to talk to.

JOHN

You're having troubles of your own, I take it.

MARY

Not exactly. Just puzzled, that's all. I have to make up my
mind about something and I don't know what to do about
it. You see—

(*Breaking off*)

This is perfectly silly! You don't go around spilling yourself to total strangers. Not if you grew up in New England,
you don't.

JOHN

Well, my God, I've just been baring my soul to you! Anyhow, I thought we decided that we're related. Has this
got something to do with Ormont?

MARY

How did you guess that?

JOHN

Oh, just from the way you reacted when I first mentioned
his name.

MARY

He's offered me a job—a good part in a good play. Just
the chance I've been waiting for. Oh, but I didn't tell! you
that I'm an actress.

JOHN

I figured that out for myself.

MARY

Well, that's more than the managers seem able to do.

JOHN

But you just said that Ormont has—

MARY

Yes. But if I take the job— You see, I've worked for him before and I know what he's like. Besides, he practically told me so. That's all.

JOHN

I see. And you don't feel that way about him.

MARY

No, I couldn't possibly ever! But, if I turn this down, I just don't know how I'm going to get along—and I'm beginning to think that maybe I'm crazy to attach so much importance to certain ideas of my own about things.

JOHN

Well, I don't see how a man can help a girl decide a thing like that. But if you don't mind my saying so, I don't like it at all—the idea of you and Ormont. You're not the type.

MARY

Thanks.

(*Suddenly*)

Well, let's not talk about that any more!

JOHN

But, look—

MARY

No, please! No more! Do you really mean you think there's no hope for anybody in New York—that we all might as well give up and go home?

JOHN

I didn't say that.

MARY

Well, that's what it sounded like.

JOHN

No, it didn't! It's like that problem of yours—something everybody has to decide for himself. All I'm saying is that New York is a tough nut that only one in a thousand can crack. And I don't seem to be that one. So, while I still have the chance, I'm going back where I belong, back among the people I know, where I can see the shape of my environment and find myself a place in it.

MARY

You mean you'd really rather spend the rest of your life selling Chevrolets to small-town folks than be here where things are happening, here in the world of art and the theater and all the great things of life?

JOHN

Not if I can be a part of it. But I've been here over two years now and I'm still on the outside looking in. And I say it's better to have a small identity of your own on Main Street than to be an anonymous pedestrian on the avenues of Manhattan.

MARY

But maybe if you stayed a little while longer, things would begin breaking your way.

JOHN

No, I've made up my mind. Listen, would you do something for me? We haven't known each other very long and I guess I have no right to ask it of you. But we seem to understand each other pretty well.

MARY

Well, what is it?

JOHN

Well, it's that fifty dollars. I'll need about half of it to get me back to Iowa. But that still leaves twenty-five or so. I've been thinking that I'd like to have one big blow-out on my last night in New York. Cocktails in some fancy bar, dinner at the Waldorf or the Plaza, orchestra seats for some good show. All the things I've always wanted to do, but have never been able to afford. Only it wouldn't be much fun doing them alone and I don't know anybody I care enough about to ask. Will you come along and keep me company?

MARY

No, I won't!

JOHN

Why not?

MARY

Because I think a person like you—young and creative and with everything to live for—has no right to get discouraged and quit. I think you should be ashamed of yourself for running away like this. I know it's none of my business, but I just can't help saying what I think.

JOHN

And will you be ashamed of yourself for giving in to Ormont?

MARY

I'm *not* giving in to Ormont!

JOHN

You've decided that?

MARY

Yes, I have!

JOHN

Well, that's an important decision.

THE SIGHTSEEING GUIDE

(*Coming up the stairs*)

All right, folks! It won't be long now!

JOHN

Tourists! Look, we could sit at one of those tables, down there, and have a Coca-Cola. That would only cost a dime.

MARY

Well, I'm willing to go that far with you.

JOHN

Thanks. All right, let's go.

THE GUIDE

Don't give up, folks! The first hundred steps are the easiest.

(*Ten or twelve* SIGHTSEERS *arrive on the platform puffing and panting and uttering complaints and expressions of fatigue.*)

MARY

Oh, it looks much worse going down!

JOHN

Wait a minute! Let me go first.

MARY

Oh, thanks!

(*They disappear.*)

THE GUIDE

Yes, I guess everybody made the grade. Now here we are, right up in the head of the statue, one hundred and fifty-one feet above the foot, two hundred and ninety-three feet above the base of the pedestal. Note the lady's hair right above you. She had a permanent in 1884 and hasn't had one since. Now from here, folks, you get a bird's-eye panorama view of New York Harbor and the lower city—

(*The* TOURISTS *have thronged to the windows, many of them with cameras leveled.* THE GUIDE *goes on talking, as the*

Curtain Falls

Scene 10

A one-room apartment, in a renovated brownstone front house in Chelsea. It is a fairly large room, containing a wide bed, a chest of drawers, several chairs, a table on which is a portable typewriter, etc. The entrance door is at the left and, at the right, a folding screen conceals the kitchenette. At the rise of the curtain, MARY, wearing a house smock over her dress, is spreading a tablecloth on a folding table, which has been set up in the middle of the room. She goes behind the screen, reappears with dishes and cutlery and begins setting the table for two. There is a knock at the door.

MARY

Come in.

(MRS. WILLIAMS, *a faded woman of forty, enters.*)

MRS. WILLIAMS

Good evening.

MARY

Oh, good evening, Mrs. Williams.

MRS. WILLIAMS

I hope I'm not disturbing you. If your supper is waiting, I can come back later.

MARY

Oh, goodness, no! I haven't even started to cook it.

MRS. WILLIAMS

Well, I don't like to be bothering you again but—

MARY

Yes, I know. How much behind are we?

MRS. WILLIAMS

Well, it's over two weeks now. I hate to be after you all the time, like this. But it's not easy for me to make both ends meet.

MARY

Well, heavens, we should pay our rent regularly, and our only excuse is that things haven't been too easy for us, either.

MRS. WILLIAMS

Oh, I know that you're honest, hard-working young people and that things just haven't been coming your way. But I'm having my hands full, putting my boys through high school, so they'll be fitted for something better than working as day laborers. If you could just let me have a little something on account—

MARY

All right, Mrs. Williams, I will.

(*She takes up her handbag and opens it.*)

Let me see now. I could pay you five dollars—yes, I think I can spare six. I have two radio engagements for next week and then we can get all caught up. Is that all right?

MRS. WILLIAMS

Yes, of course it is. I'm very thankful to you. Good night.

MARY

Good night, Mrs. Williams. And we'll try not to let it happen again.

(MRS. WILLIAMS *exits.* MARY *takes out a little memorandum book and makes an entry, then resumes setting the table. There is a knock at the door.*)

Come in.

(ORMONT *enters*.)

ORMONT

Hello, Mary. I hope I'm intruding.

MARY

(*Looking at him in astonishment*)

Why, good evening. It's nice to see you again.

ORMONT

You remember me? Lawrence Ormont—the wolf of Broadway.

MARY

Yes, I never forget a face. Take off your sheep's clothing and sit down, won't you?

ORMONT

(*Removing his overcoat*)

A nice domestic atmosphere you have here.

MARY

Yes, I think so, too.

ORMONT

Let me answer the questions that are trembling on your lips. How did I get your address? Equity—the labor union of the unemployed. What brought me here? A Parmelee cab.

MARY

Well, I'm glad of that. It's a long walk from Broadway.

ORMONT

You goddam little fool, why did you turn down that part in *White Magic?*

MARY

I wrote you why.

ORMONT

You had other plans! What plans?

MARY

Oh, just different things I wanted to do.

ORMONT

Since then I wrote three letters to your last address, asking you to come in to see me. And I'm a guy who has made himself famous by asking people *not* to come to see him. I know you got them because they didn't come back. Unless the Gestapo intercepted them.

MARY

I did get them. I always leave a forwarding address when I move.

ORMONT

I'm just the opposite. I frequently move in order to avoid getting letters. Why haven't you been in?

MARY

I've been busy.

ORMONT

Doing what?

MARY

Oh, all sorts of things. I've had a few radio jobs and—

ORMONT

Radio jobs! What's the matter?—don't they employ women in the Street Cleaning Department? Do you know that *White Magic* is a smash?

MARY

Yes, I do! And I want to congratulate you. I was lucky enough to get a dollar seat for a Wednesday matinee and I've never been more thrilled in my life. It's a beautiful

play and, if you don't mind my saying so, I think you've
done a simply marvelous job of direction.

ORMONT

Well, I still think it's good. I suppose you know that
Laura Woodward, who's playing the part I offered you,
has scored heavily, and that every time she turns on a
faucet a Hollywood scout comes out.

MARY

Well, she certainly deserves it. I thought she was swell.

ORMONT

Have you taken up Christian Science or are you giving
me the run-around?

MARY

Is there anything wrong about being glad that somebody
has made a success?

ORMONT

When one actress rejoices in another's success, God becomes restive. Take my advice and don't monkey with the
Divine Plan. If you'd taken that part, you'd be making a
hundred and fifty a week and you'd be on your way to
the top. Have you ever thought of that?

MARY

Yes. Frequently.

ORMONT

Regretfully, I hope.

MARY

No.

ORMONT

No? Listen, let's understand each other. What the hell do
you think I've come here for?

MARY

I didn't think it would be polite to ask you.

ORMONT

You know who I am, don't you?

MARY

Yes. You introduced yourself when you came in.

ORMONT

I don't have to go hunting for actresses in the rabbit warrens of Chelsea. All I have to do is whisper: "I want an actress," and an hour later it becomes necessary to call out the riot squad.

MARY

I know that, too.

ORMONT

All right. Then let's get down to cases. I'm getting ready to do another play. Do you want to be in it?

MARY

I'd love to be in it. Only—

ORMONT

Only what?

MARY

Well, I'd want to be sure that it's just for the part that you want me.

ORMONT

No girl who works for me could ever be sure of that. Particularly you.

MARY

Yes, that's what I thought.

ORMONT

I don't have to come to Chelsea to look for sleeping partners, either.

MARY

No, I'm sure you don't.

ORMONT

Then why do I?

MARY

I can't imagine.

ORMONT

Goddam it, you little nitwit, don't you know when a man is interested in you?

MARY

Well, I guess I'm a funny girl that way, Mr. Ormont. But I don't like a man's interests to be quite so general.

ORMONT

Listen, Goldilocks, I'm a fellow who always takes no for an answer, because there are never less than six girls waiting in my outer office. Nobody expects intelligence in an actress, but even you should be able to understand that I wouldn't be here if I weren't serious. What the hell do you want—marriage? All right, by God, I'll marry you.

MARY

You're asking me to marry you?

ORMONT

Do you want my lawyer to draw up a notarized proposal with a certified copy of my divorce decree attached? I'm a busy man, sweetheart. When I cross Ninth Avenue to ask a girl to marry me, you damn well know that history is being made.

MARY

Well, I must admit that I feel flattered.

ORMONT

And well you may. We'll need a license. Tomorrow morning?

MARY

No.

ORMONT

Tomorrow afternoon?

MARY

I meant no to the proposal.

ORMONT

You're turning me down?

MARY

Yes, Mr. Ormont, I am.

ORMONT

Maybe I haven't made myself clear. I am offering to make you my wife. Mrs. Lawrence Ormont. I am offering you a wedding ring—platinum with diamonds—to show to your Aunt Prudence and the Governor of New Hampshire. I am offering you a career, clothes, a car, a home where you don't have to sleep in the kitchen and the bathroom is in the same building.

MARY

Those are all wonderful things and I hope I'll have them some day, before I'm too old to enjoy them. But if I don't, why I don't, that's all.

ORMONT

You're sitting here, in a bungalow apron, waiting for Mr. Right to come along?

MARY

Not any more, I'm not.

ORMONT

Don't be cryptic, darling. It doesn't go with your legs.

(*Suddenly, looking at the table*)

Good God! Tiffin for two! Please don't tell me that I've stumbled into a love nest!

MARY

That's exactly what you've done.

ORMONT

No!

(*Walking about the room*)

So you've succumbed to the blandishments of some small-time Lancelot. And he's set you up in style among the clotheslines and the chimney pots.

MARY

We're happy.

ORMONT

And for how long?

MARY

For as long as we love each other. That might be forever—who knows?

ORMONT

I know. Until the end of the sixth package of soap flakes. You can't mix love and dishwater. Where did you discover this impecunious Romeo?

MARY

On top of the Statue of Liberty.

ORMONT

That's a glamorous trysting place. What is he—an unemployed parachute jumper?

MARY

He's a writer. A very good one, too, who just hasn't had the right breaks yet. He's been to see you, several times, though of course, you wouldn't remember him. I suppose it *is* hard for you to understand how we can be so happy with so little.

(*As* JOHN *enters, with a package of flowers, she goes to him and kisses him.*)

Hello, darling.

JOHN

Hello, dear.

ORMONT

O, my prophetic soul, my uncle!

JOHN

(*In amazement, as he sees* ORMONT)

Why, hello, Mr. Ormont!

ORMONT

So it's you!

JOHN

(*Puzzled*)

Why? Were you expecting someone else?

MARY

Flowers, darling? Why?

JOHN

Oh, just on the strength of my getting the job.

MARY

Have you got a job?

JOHN

Say, what is this? Hasn't Mr. Ormont told you?

MARY

No! What?

JOHN

Why, he took me on today as his play-reader.

MARY

Oh, how wonderful!

JOHN

Yes, I think so, too.

(*To* ORMONT)

It's just like you not to tell her.

ORMONT

Yes, I'm a comical fellow.

MARY

Mr. Ormont came to see me about something else. He didn't know about you and me until just now.

ORMONT

(*To* JOHN)

Why in hell didn't *you* tell *me?*

JOHN

Well, there didn't seem to be any occasion for it. It never occurred to me that you'd be even remotely interested in my domestic life.

ORMONT

Sit down, both of you.

(*Wonderingly, they seat themselves on the bed.* ORMONT *takes a chair.*)

To me, this is a phenomenon that merits investigation. You're in love with each other?

JOHN

That's an understatement.

ORMONT

No wisecracks. I'm doing the talking.

JOHN

Sorry. But it's still an understatement.

ORMONT

You're starving and you love each other.

MARY

We're not starving. I was just getting dinner ready.

JOHN

But if we were, you'd still be right.

MARY

Yes.

ORMONT

How long is it since you both came in to see me for the first time?

JOHN

About two and a half years, I guess.

MARY

Yes, just about.

ORMONT

A couple of the greenest yokels I ever saw. Idiot innocence in your eyes and corn silk in your hair.

JOHN

That's certainly an accurate description of what I was like.

MARY

Me, too.

ORMONT

And now you're New Yorkers, living on husks in a West Side rookery. And getting nowhere.

JOHN

Don't forget I have a job with you.

MARY

And I hope to have one, some day soon.

ORMONT

Lawrence Ormont. *Deus ex machina.* To hell with that! You must have something in yourselves, and that's what interests me. You've been high-hatted, stepped on, pushed around—right?

JOHN

Yes. Plenty.

ORMONT

And still you're not discouraged?

MARY

No, we're not a bit discouraged.

JOHN

We did hit some pretty low spots in the course of our checkered careers. But all that kicking around you talk about has helped us to grow up, I guess. We've learned to take it. And it's made us good and tough.

ORMONT

Yes, that's it! You've put your finger on it! Tough! That's New York. If it doesn't kill you, it makes you tough.

MARY

You forgot one thing. It's easier for two to be tough, than for just one. If we'd had to keep going, all alone—well, I don't know.

ORMONT

Yes, it's easier for two. I'm making four thousand dollars a week and it means nothing to me. What are you having for dinner?

MARY

Cream of tomato soup, pork and beans and stewed pears. All out of tin cans.

ORMONT

All right. I'll stay.

(*He takes up his hat and coat.*)

JOHN

(*Surprised*)

You're not leaving, are you?

(ORMONT *exits.*)

Do you think he'll be back?

MARY

I don't know. But we'd better set another place, anyhow.

JOHN

I'll do it.

(*He goes behind the screen as* MARY *unwraps the flowers.*)

MARY

Oh, lovely! Thank you, darling!

(*As* JOHN *reappears, she kisses him.*)

Here, I'll set the place. You fix the flowers.

(JOHN *goes behind the screen.*)

JOHN

What did Ormont come here for?

MARY

I'll tell you later. It's sort of a long story. I want to hear about your job. I'm so excited about it.

JOHN

(*Appearing with the flowers in a vase*)

Yes, it's kind of a lifesaver, isn't it?

MARY

It certainly is. And, what's more, it means that at last you're in the theater, instead of doing one of those awful grimy jobs again.

JOHN

Yes, if I can't write plays that anybody reads, I can at least read plays that anybody writes.

MARY

And now he'll be sure to read your new play when you get it finished.

JOHN

Yes, and I intend to give him a very favorable report on it. You haven't asked about the salary.

MARY

I haven't dared.

JOHN

Thirty-five a week.

MARY

Why, how marvelous! We can live in state on that.

JOHN

Well, at least, we can keep abreast of the rent and go to the Newsreel Theater, once a month. Mary darling—

MARY

What?

JOHN

I think we should get married now.

MARY

Do you, darling?

JOHN

Yes, I do. Will you marry me?

MARY

Well, I just turned down one proposal, and, after all, I don't want to die an old maid.

JOHN

Ormont asked you to marry him?

MARY

Uh-huh. All the boys are after me. Oh, darling, hold me tight!

(*He embraces her.* Ormont *enters with a bottle wrapped in paper.*)

ORMONT

Wonderful shops in this neighborhood. I think I'll come over here to do my marketing.

(*He unwraps the bottle.*)

MARY

Champagne!

ORMONT

Pork and beans without champagne—unthinkable!

MARY

Roses and champagne! Why it's a gala!

ORMONT

I hope you don't mind it being in a bottle. They didn't have any in tin cans.

MARY

Well, I'll get dinner started.

(*To* JOHN)

Oh, darling, invite Mr. Ormont to our wedding.

JOHN

Yes, Mr. Ormont, and maybe you'll be the best man.

ORMONT

My boy, I always have been.

Curtain

Scene 11

Two taxis face left. The Driver *at the right is* Kaltbart. *In the cab at the left is* Brodsky. *Beside him is some smartlooking luggage and next to the cab are three* News Photographers, *waiting with ready cameras. As the curtain rises,* John *and* Mary *appear at the right and approach* Kaltbart's *cab.* Mary *is wearing a new dress and a new hat and a corsage of gardenias.* John *has a flower in his buttonhole. He carries two small suitcases.*

JOHN

Get in!
  (*As they enter the cab*)
Grand Central Station, please.

KALTBART

Yes, sir.

MARY

  (*Leaning back*)
Two taxi rides in one day. Why, it's a life of luxury.

JOHN

It certainly is.

MARY

Don't start spoiling me, darling.

JOHN

Don't worry, I won't. Our budget allows us twenty cents a day for transportation.

MARY

What's more, it's my first trip outside the city, except one Christmas visit to Daddy.

JOHN

Same here.

MARY

We're really being terribly extravagant. New clothes—and this trip!

JOHN

I know. But it's not really legal without Niagara Falls. And I guess neither of us will be getting married very often.

MARY

You don't think so?

JOHN

No, I don't.

(*He kisses her. There is a stir of activity among the photographers, as* DOROTHY CLARK *appears at the left on the arm of* FREDERIC WINTHROP. BRODSKY *opens the door of the cab, and, as they enter it, the cameras click.* DOROTHY *and* WINTHROP *settle into the seat and the* PHOTOGRAPHERS *go away.*)

BRODSKY

Grand Central?

WINTHROP

Yes, please.

DOROTHY

Now how did those cameramen ever track us down here to City Hall? Honestly, Fred, I have no private life, at all.

BRODSKY

It's the penalty of fame.

WINTHROP

Well, think how much worse a big church wedding would have been.

DOROTHY

Oh, I just couldn't have gone through another one of those! I loved being married by the judge, without any of that kneeling and all those awful flowers that give you a sick headache. Only I thought they always wear robes.

WINTHROP

Only when they're on the bench. Do you know, I've never been to Niagara Falls.

DOROTHY

Oh, I have. But never on a honeymoon.

WINTHROP

Well, I suppose we really should have gone somewhere else. But I have so little time to spare, and with the C.I.O. convention in Buffalo, it seemed the most practical place to go.

DOROTHY

Oh, I think it was a marvelous idea! I'm terribly excited about going to the convention.

WINTHROP

Yes, there'll be important labor leaders from all over the country and a lot of serious problems to discuss.

DOROTHY

Yes, it sounds simply fascinating. Tell me again what C.I.O. stands for, darling.

WINTHROP

Congress of Industrial Organization.

DOROTHY

I *must* remember that. And what's the other one—the one we're against?

WINTHROP

A.F. of L. The American Federation of Labor.

DOROTHY

Yes, they're those awful reactionaries. I get furious every time I think of them.

WINTHROP

It's only the leaders. The rank and file are all right.

DOROTHY

Oh, I'm not saying anything against the rank and file. But those leaders! What are we going to do about them?

WINTHROP

Dear, I can't tell you how happy I am, that you're really getting vitally interested in the movement.

DOROTHY

Interested! Why, I've never been so thrilled about anything in my life.

(WINTHROP *kisses her.*)

MARY

I'll never forget my first ride from Grand Central. I just sat and gaped. I didn't believe I could ever possibly be even a tiny part of it. And now it's all beginning to look like home. Darling, I love New York.

JOHN

So do I! I hate the damned place! But, God, how I love it!

MARY

Let's never live anywhere else.

JOHN

That's all right with me. Do you think we'll ever make a dent in it?

MARY

Of course we will! Look I've got it all figured out. One night—let's see, one, two, three, four, five years from now, the limousines are going to draw up in front of a theater, and the top hats and ermine capes are going to fight their way through the little autograph pests, and on the marquee, it's going to say: "Mary Ward in *Golden Moments,* a new play by John Thompson."

JOHN

(*Putting his arms around her*)

You know what I think? I think you're a little crazy in the head.

MARY

Well, maybe a little. But it's such fun, darling!

(*He kisses her.*)

BRODSKY

Factionalism! That's what's wrong with the revolutionary movement.

WINTHROP

Yes, you're quite right about that.

DOROTHY

Oh, is he? Well, what are we doing about it, darling?

WINTHROP

Well, we're trying to correct it. But it's not a simple problem.

DOROTHY

I'm beginning to think there just aren't any simple problems.

(BRODSKY'S *cab stops and a* REDCAP *unloads the luggage, as* WINTHROP *and* DOROTHY *get out and he pays* BRODSKY.)

BRODSKY

Thanks and *mazeltov*. That means good luck in the Jewish language.

DOROTHY

Oh, thanks! I must remember that. Molotov!

WINTHROP

(*To the* REDCAP)

The six-forty to Niagara Falls.

(*He and* DOROTHY *exit, followed by the* REDCAP. BRODSKY *switches on his radio, and we hear the Mendelssohn Wedding March.*)

MARY

Darling, there's one thing that's on my mind.

JOHN

Thank you, darling.

MARY

It's about that first night. If I'm on the stage and you're in some bar around the corner, who's going to look after little Edward?

JOHN

Little who?

MARY

Little Edward.

JOHN

Is that somebody I should know?

MARY

It certainly is. Though they say it's a wise father that

knows his own child. Of course, he'll be about four-and-a-half by then and—

JOHN

Excuse me, but I'm not following this conversation.

MARY

Well, darling, now that you've made an honest woman of me, I think it's safe to tell you.

JOHN

No!

MARY

Yes.

(*The taxi stops and a* REDCAP *appears at the right and takes their bags.*)

JOHN

But—

MARY

Grand Central Station, darling.

JOHN

But—

(*He steps out of the cab.* MARY *follows him.*)

MARY

Pay the driver, darling.

JOHN

Oh, yes.

(*He hands* KALTBART *a bill.*)

Keep the change!

KALTBART

Thank you very much. And good luck to you both. In Vienna, I was an actor, also!

MARY

Oh, were you! Well, good luck to *you!*

(*To the* REDCAP)

The six-forty to Niagara Falls.

JOHN

(*As they follow the* REDCAP *off*)

You mean we're going to be the parents of a native New York?

MARY

Why, of course! I hadn't thought of that!

(KALTBART *switches on his radio and a swing version of the Lohengrin Wedding March is heard. A* BOY *with a suitcase appears at the right and enters* KALTBART'S *cab.*)

THE BOY

The Young Men's Christian Association, please.

KALTBART

Yes, sir.

(A GIRL *with a suitcase appears at the left and enters* BRODSKY'S *cab.*)

BRODSKY

What destination?

THE GIRL

Do you know where the Young Women's Hebrew Association is?

BRODSKY

I certainly do. A very intimate friend of mine used to live there. She's married now and residing in Bay Ridge.

(*Both cabs are in motion and the wedding marches swell higher. A carillon of church bells chimes in as the curtain falls.*)

CURTAIN